LORCA'S
ROMANCERO GITANO

For Joyce

H. RAMSDEN

LORCA'S
ROMANCERO GITANO

EIGHTEEN COMMENTARIES

MANCHESTER UNIVERSITY PRESS
Manchester and New York

Distributed exclusively in the USA and Canada
by St. Martin's Press Inc.,
175 Fifth Avenue, New York, NY10010, USA

© H. Ramsden 1988

First published 1988
by Manchester University Press,
Oxford Road, Manchester M13 9PL, UK
and St. Martin's Press Inc.,
Room 400, 175 Fifth Avenue, New York, NY 10010, USA

British Library cataloguing in publication data
Ramsden, H.
  Lorca's Romancero gitano: eighteen commentaries.
  I. García Lorca, Federico. Romancero gitano
  I. Title
  861'. 62   PQ6613.A763P763

Library of Congress cataloging in publication data
Ramsden, H. (Herbert)
  Lorca's Romancero gitano: eighteen commentaries/H. Ramsden.
    p.   cm.
  Bibliography: p. 123.
  ISBN 0-7190-2848-5: $35.00 (U.S.: est.).   ISBN 0-7190-2849-3
  (pbk.): $10.00 (U.S.: est.)
    1. García Lorca, Federico, 1898–1936.   Primer romancero gitano.
  I. Title.
  PQ6613.A763P7637   1988
  861'.62 — dc 19   87-38263

ISBN 0 7190 2848 5 *hardback*
     0 7190 2849 3 *paper*

Typeset in Hong Kong
by Best-set Typesetter Ltd

Printed in Great Britain
by Biddles Ltd, Guildford and King's Lynn

CONTENTS

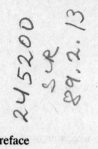

PREFACE

Romancero gitano is the most widely celebrated and commented book of poetry in Spanish literature. Despite its difficulty it is also a favourite with students at all levels. The present poem-by-poem guide was written, over a period of twenty-five years, principally for students at the University of Manchester but also as a hobby and a means of relaxation from more onerous commitments. Publication for a wider public has been finally prompted by three considerations: the overwhelming amount of critical material published on the book and the need for some form of guidance to it, the relative neglect or misunderstanding of certain poems, and the conviction that one should counter with Lorcan 'pies de plomo' a recent tendency to eccentric interpretation. A comprehensive collection of commentaries, it seemed, would be useful both for students and teachers and perhaps also, in certain cases at least, for the Lorca specialist. With each poem I offer a brief introduction to relevant background material, a fairly comprehensive commentary, a brief reference to strikingly divergent critical views and a select critical bibliography.

Unlike some of the most notable writers on the work I do not emphasise a single interpretative approach. My aim has been to immerse myself totally in each successive poem and to indicate whatever I find most relevant to appreciation, with emphasis not only on the poem's successive parts but also, very especially, on the manner of their interaction and integration into a dynamically progressing whole. It is here especially that I hope to have made a positive contribution to a better understanding of *Romancero gitano*. Critics have generally come to accept that mere narrative plays little part in most of the poems, but adverse consequences have often ensued. For example, much attention has been paid to individual images, but relatively little, even in commentaries, to demonstrating the function of those images in the total context of the poem. It is as though critics were giving tacit support to the opinion of the work's least enthusiastic contemporary reviewer, Andrenio: magical 'materiales poéticos' but with a notable lack of order, discipline and 'elaboración'; 'Lo que le falta a este poeta es atender a la composición, desarrollar el arte constructivo.' This is far from being my own view and one of my aims in this work is to refute such criticism. In doing so, I shall be refuting also the occasional suggestion that Lorca's work is 'deshumanizada'.

The poems' lack of clear narrative progression and the associated emphasis on imagery has led to a further unfortunate consequence. Prompted, perhaps, by a desire for intellectual order and intelligible patterns, some critics have tended to impose on Lorca's work a structure that individual poems seem to deny. This has revealed itself principally in two ways. On the one hand there has been a tendency to impose mechanistic equations as though these were valid for all Lorca's poems — and, indeed, for all his writings — and certain commentaries consist largely of parallels with other passages taken from wholly different contexts. I believe this to be unhelpful and even misleading. The moon, for example, is clearly malevolent in 'Romance de la luna, luna' (relevant popular tradition and the poem itself make this clear), but I find it inappropriate to apply this equation also — as has been done — to those delightful lines from 'La casada infiel', *ni los cristales con luna / relumbran con ese brillo*. Here again my own emphasis is on the *immediate* context and what is suggested by that context. Passages from elsewhere in Lorca's work are often revealing, but, where I myself use them, I hope it is with discretion. The other form of structure that is occasionally imposed on Lorca's poems comes entirely from outside his work. Attempted interpretations in the light of depth psychology offer the clearest example. Here nothing is safe. Anything that sticks up is liable to be seen as a breast or a phallic symbol; anything that recedes or encloses, as a womb symbol. As literary criticism aimed at the fuller appreciation of individual poems I find this unhelpful and even pernicious. But here as elsewhere the reader will be able to judge for himself by reference to the brief critical observations with which I conclude each commentary and by appropriate consideration of the studies referred to.

My main aim, I repeat, is to study each poem as a self-contained and coherently integrated work of art. But having read several hundred commentaries on poems from *Romancero gitano* without finding any that can by considered even remotely definitive, I am far from claiming definitiveness for any of my own commentaries and the reader will doubtless discover many weaknesses: lines that I have misunderstood or not explained adequately, relevant references and resonances that I have overlooked, poems in which I have failed to see the magical progression with which Lorca replaced mere narrative, relevant bibliography that I should have known and did not .... But on many points, I believe, my commentaries mark a clear advance on existing criticism and after many years of hesitation I have finally decided that publication is justified. Doubtless, if I had held on to my typescript for another ten or twenty years, it would have become better, for during the past two decades almost no month has passed without some form of rewriting and improvement. But in the last five years at least changes have been minimal and my study has perhaps reached a stage where others, in the light of their own experience and responses, can add more than I can. I offer the work, then, as a drawing together and development of much that has been done on *Romancero gitano*, as a provisional guide to more sensitive reading of the poems and, hopefully, as a sound working basis for fellow enthusiasts who wish and feel able to go further in the elucidation and appreciation of this remarkable poetry. In a substantial introduction to my edition of *Romancero gitano* I seek to draw my main findings together into the sort of overall synthesis that the present study necessarily lacks.

1988 H R

1
ROMANCE DE LA LUNA, LUNA

Romancero gitano, said Lorca, begins with two invented myths: that of
the moon as a dancer of death and that of the wind as a satyr. It is the
former with which we are here concerned. The moon comes down to
the gypsy forge and carries away a child who is there alone. The theme
is not wholly Lorca's invention. As in many of his *romances* he starts
from a specific event, legend or superstition; in this case a superstition.
Emilio Castelar referred to it in a book published ten years before
Lorca's birth. Through some 'misteriosísima superstición', he wrote,
nursemaids used to warn their young charges against looking too much
at the moon, 'pues recordábanse casos de haber bajado a comerse y
tragarse los niños mirones' (*Galería histórica de mujeres célebres*, I,
Madrid 1888, pp. 33–4). The moon, then, as a bringer of death — and
especially as a bringer of death to children who look at it too much — is
part of popular tradition, and Lorca himelf emphasised the role played
by peasant nursemaids and servants in transmitting popular culture to
the children of wealthier families such as that of his own parents.

But — and again this is typical of Lorca's writing — the specific
reference has wider resonances. Behind the child-eating moon referred
to by Castelar is the mythical moon of primitive cultures, ominous and
threatening. Angel Alvarez de Miranda, an authority on primitive
religions, has studied the subject at length. To primitive man the moon,
with its monthly cycle of birth, growth, decline and death, was a reflection of human life; also, by extension, an influence on human life
and a bringer of death:

> Para la religiosidad primitiva y arcaica la luna contiene en sí a la
> muerte, la sufre y la trasciende. Luna y muerte son inseparables:
> la luna es su dueña y su símbolo. Por eso existe toda una categoría
> de mitos primitivos destinados a 'explicar' el origen de la muerte
> en los que la luna es presentada como fautora, inventora y dis-
> tribuidora de la muerte (*La metáfora y el mito*, Madrid 1963,
> p. 41).

Other scholars, most notably Blanquat, have pointed to the possibility
of more recondite sources for the poem, though it is not certain, or

necessary to assume, that Lorca was aware of them. In less rationally regimented areas of society the magic of legend, myth and superstition lives on into the present and Lorca referred in lectures to the two areas most relevant to this poem: that of the gypsy and that of the child. It is Lorca's merit — one of his merits — to have felt the magic and mystery of primitive superstitions and to have recreated it for the sophisticated reader of the present and future.

At this point we come to the poet's own invention, for what he does in his 'invented myth' is to present the moon's action in dance terms appropriate to Andalusia: 'mito de la luna sobre tierras de danza dramática, Andalucía interior concentrada y religiosa' (III, 342). The last words are important, especially for readers who may associate Andalusian dancing too readily with the uncontrolled contortions that are commonly offered to tourists. Traditional Andalusian dancing operates from within a framework of ritual, like oriental dancing, and it is the ritualistic aspect that Lorca emphasises in his poem. '¡Qué baile de amor y frío!', he wrote in an early draft of the poem (*A* I, 138). Love and seduction, but also icy detachment. It is a duality that he develops throughout the moon's dance.[1]

The poem first appeared in 1926 under the title 'Romance de la luna de los gitanos'.[2] The revised title is less anecdotic and, with repeated *luna* and associated lulling sounds and rhythms, more incantatory and

---

[1] In fact it is not only tourists who are now offered degenerate forms of Andalusian dancing. Since writing the above I have noted the following lament by an authority on Andalusian popular culture:

Aquel 'no descomponer pelo ni rostro' de las grandes bailaoras, aquella serenidad de figura y majestad de cabeza y brazos, tan olvidados hoy, son formas residuales apolíneas de la danza india. La descomposición de la figura, las contorsiones bruscas, la furia dinámica a que el baile flamenco ha sido arrastrado en la actualidad, revelan otros influjos, el americano principalmente, con lo que se ha 'modernizado' a costa de la fidelidad a su milenaria esencia (Ricardo Molina, *Misterios del arte flamenco*, Barcelona 1967, p. 193).

[2] *El Norte de Castilla* (Valladolid), 9 April 1926; republished under the same title in *Verso y Prosa* (Murcia), no. 7, July 1927. I disregard the earlier but so far untraced publication of the poem in *Proa* of Buenos Aires, referred to by José Mora Guarnido (*FGL y su mundo*, Buenos Aires 1958, p. 210). An autograph version dated 29 July 1924 (*A* I, 138–41) has no title; another autograph version, apparently written in February 1926, bears the title 'Romance gitano de la luna luna de los gitanos' (III, 747).

magical. In an Andalusian context the work *fragua* in the first line of the poem is sufficient to retain the gypsy connection.

1–8. The moon, in her white dress, has come down to the gypsy forge. The child, heedless of traditional warnings 'de no mirar a la luna mucho' (Castelar, p. 33), looks and looks, fascinated and apparently transfixed (incantatory repetition of sounds, especially *i* and nasal consonants, and of words; variation on repetition, too, in *mira / está mirando*; an overall impression of enchantment and yearning). In the disturbed air (not just physically disturbed, *removido*, but emotionally moved, *conmovido*) the moon dances her ritualistic dance 'de amor y frío', with a subtle interplay of seduction (flowers, dance-like movement of arms, bared breasts) and emotional detachment (whiteness, coldness, hardness). The duality is summed up in *lúbrica y pura*: the moon, sinuously seductive (*lubricious*) in her dance, is also detached and pure.[3] In autographs of the poem (*A* I, 139–40; *OC* III, 747–8) line 1 has *viene* instead of *vino*. This is consistent with the ensuing present tenses and suggests a purely narrative progression. But the subsequent change to *vino* was masterly, for it involved three improvements: the sound of the vowel (more in harmony with the incantatory *i* and nasal sounds of lines 3–4); a pointer to time elapsed between the moon's arrival and the child's trance-like fascination; finally and perhaps especially, the establishment between poem and reader of a duality comparable to that between moon and child: on the one hand a series of present tenses (3–8) that bring the action seductively close to us (cf. 'amor', *lúbrica*); on the other hand the opening preterite which suggests a more contoured subject and gives

---

[3] *Lúbrica* is most commonly translated and interpreted as *lascivious* (even as *lewd*), with possible over-emphasis on the contrast with *pure* (cf. Campbell's 'lascivious yet pure'). In fact, *lúbrica* itself contains suggestions of emotional detachment, partly because it is a learned word (and therefore not conducive to emotional involvement), partly because of its complexity of meaning (*seductive*, *evasive*, *slippery*, almost *snake-like*).

    Cf. El propio Vespasiano, en su facha, maneras y conducta, era evasivo, resbaladizo, escurridizo, seductor, como una sierpe irisada (A poseer Herminia algún rudimento de latín, cosa que maldita la falta que le hacía y le hubiera sentado como a un Santo Cristo un par de pistolas, en vez de aplicar a Vespasiano estos cuatro calificativos, se hubiera servido de una palabra que los resume todos: lúbrico) (Ramón Pérez de Ayala, *Tigre Juan*, Madrid 1926, pp. 242–3).

mythical distance to the whole event (cf. 'frío', *pura*). We are touching on a duality that is basic to Lorca's poetic art.

9–20.   Dialogue. The child, still under the moon's spell (suggested by the dark sounds and incantatory repetition in line 9), seems concerned rather than threatening in his warning of what would happen if the gypsies came. They would make white rings and necklaces of the moon's heart, a reminder both of a gypsy craft, the making of trinkets, and of the moon's own unfeeling whiteness, even of the heart. But the moon is not afraid. She wants only to dance. When the gypsies come, she says, the child will lie on the anvil with his eyes closed. The pace quickens as the gypsies draw near (*ya siento sus caballos*, with progression from the earlier *Si vinieran, Cuando vengan*), and the eight-line exchange of 9–16 gives way to a more feverish four-line exchange (17–20), with a more varied range of vowels (18), a more fractured rhythm (19), a subtle shift in the meaning of *déjame* (earlier *let me* [*dance*]; now *leave me* [*alone*]) and an associated suggestion that the child is trying to push the moon away, since he treads on her starched dress. But the starched whiteness is not merely physical description. Like the earlier white heart it reminds us also of the moon's lack of feeling. In *Canciones* the desolation of autumn had produced a similar effect on the poet and prompted similar imagery: 'pecho almidonado [. . .], corazón de cera' (I, 332). In view of Lorca's emphasis on the moon's lack of warmth — hard, cold breasts, white heart, starched dress — one is not wholly convinced by critics' suggestions that she is presented as a mother figure, though it could conceivably be argued that she (and, through her, death itself) is seen as a substitute for the mother who is absent both from the poem and from the lives of children whose nurses, rather than mothers, warn them of the moon. One is almost surprised that no sociologist or psychologist of literature has made the point, especially in view of Lorca's reference elsewhere to the 'almidonado pecho de la nodriza' (III, 287).

21–4.   The horseman was approaching, beating the drum of the plain — with a notable combination of image, sounds and rhythm in the second line to create the effect of a galloping horse.[4] But who is *el*

---

[4] Compare Virgil's well-known and similarly onomatopoeic 'Quadrupedante putrem sonitu quatit ungula campum' (*Aeneid*, viii, 596), nicely rendered by Robert Fitzgerald as 'Hoofbeat of horses shaking the dust of the plain'.

jinete? It is tempting and usual to identify him with the approaching gypsies. But why *el jinete*? And why does Lorca here change from the repeated use of the words *los gitanos* (10, 14, 26, 34)? And why is this verse (in most editions) separated from the following verse if the subject matter is the same? And might there not be some weakness in indicating virtually the same thing twice (21, 25–6) without intensifying development? Finally and perhaps most importantly, why does the reader feel such a powerful emotive impact as he reads these lines, as though the horseman were some mysterious phantom rider? *Jinetes* in Lorca's poetry are almost invariably associated with death, either suffering it ('Canción de jinete', I, 313) or prompting it ('Diálogo del Amargo', I, 231–40). Similarly in this poem. Lorca, I feel, is not presenting a mere real-life horseman; he is suggesting a mythical herald of death. Significantly the verb *se acercaba* is less physical than *venían* (25), for example, and is therefore more readily applicable to the approach of misfortune or death. The change to the imperfect tense, too, is important: *El jinete se acercaba* does not merely describe action taking place after and separate from the dialogue; it is also relevant to the time covered by the dialogue (during which death was in fact approaching) and it leads on almost inevitably to a new present tense in which the foretold outcome has occurred and the child lies with his eyes closed.

25–8. The gypsies too were coming, bronze and dream, and the image is echoed in the following lines: with heads erect (bronze) and eyes half closed (dream). At the lowest level it is an allusion to purely physical characteristics: dark complexion and almond-shaped eyes. But physical characteristics in Lorca tend to have wider resonances: in this case, pride (the erect profile of a bronze figure; cf. his insistence elsewhere on the gypsies' *perfil*) and dreamlike qualities which Lorca associated with his basically gentle gypsies ('gitano verdadero, incapaz del mal', III, 345).

29–32. A characteristic Lorcan sense of yearning is expressed in the song of the nightjar (repeated *cómo canta; ay*; exclamation) and the moon passes across the sky with a child by the hand. The indefinite article in *un niño* is important. The link with what has gone before is suggested rather than stated. Successive scenes and images in Lorca interact by subtle resonances rather than by being causally connected as by an omniscient narrator. There is an air of mystery and magic about these lines that the definite article, too anecdotic, would destroy.

33–6. Back in the forge the gypsies' world of pride and dream has been shattered. The air that earlier was disturbed by the moon's appearance is serene again, shrouding the escaping moon. Or is it in vigil over the forge as is commonly stated? From a purely syntactical point of view one would expect *la* in lines 35 and 36 to refer to the immediately preceding *fragua*, but in the overall context of the poem one feels it refers to the moon. This feeling is encouraged especially by the parallelism between lines 3–4 and lines 35–6. The air, then, conspires with the moon in the child's death. The poem ends as it began: with a musical, spell-like incantation. This helps to frame the poem and to give lyrical distance to the tragedy that has gone before (cf. the end of *Bodas de sangre*). But it is worth considering Roy Campbell's view: 'In the last verse the gipsies come to the forge, and start weeping and giving loud cries on not finding the child, but the last verses seem to lose their force since our attention is transposed from the moon to the wind, which in its turn is supposed to be protecting and keeping guard over the moon' (*Lorca*, 42). A similar criticism has been made of the last scene of *Bodas de sangre*. One need not agree. Lorca may have been seeking a different effect from that desired by certain of his commentators. He is still a long way from the starker, more Chekhovian style of *Doña Rosita la soltera* and *La casa de Bernarda Alba*.

Published commentaries on 'Romance de la luna, luna' are in general along the lines of the above or at least not incompatible with it and Correa, in a seminal study, devotes some of his most perceptive pages to this poem, with characteristic emphasis on the interplay of anecdote and myth. Somewhat aside from mainline interpretation Ramond and Feal Deibe, in two of the longest commentaries, apply notions derived from psychoanalysis. I here illustrate by reference to Feal Deibe's study. The moon, it is suggested, is a mother figure who sets out to seduce her son. But seduction by woman is also a form of death, and the child (who represents man in his defencelessness against woman) threatens the moon with the gypsies (adult virility), to which the moon retorts that when they come the child will lie with closed eyes on the anvil (= breasts), an equation that prompts Feal Deibe to see the forge itself as a symbolic maternal prison.[5] Again the child invokes

---

[5] For further evidence of Feal Deibe's partiality to maternal prisons and wombs — and an associated error of interpretation — see FGL, *Bodas de sangre*, Manchester University Press, 1980, p. 78.

male strength (*que ya siento sus caballos*), but the moon will preserve its purity against man's sexual desire (*No pises mi blancor*). The gypsies arrive late, which together with the passivity of dream indicates defeat. The moon-mother-woman triumphs and carries away the representative of the male sex, leaving man, weeping like a child, imprisoned within the forge, having died of love — the symbolic expression of man's defeat by woman. I fail to find an obviously close relationship between Lorca's poem and Feal Deibe's commentary.

Select bibliography: J. Rivas Crespo, 'Comentario a la poesía de GL "RLL"', in *Hispania* 39 (1956), 97; H. H. Chapman, Jr., 'Two poetic techniques: Lorca's "RLL" and Goethe's "Erlkönig"', in *Hispania* 39 (1956), 450–5; Correa, 23–6; Blanquat, 376–89; C. Feal Deibe, '"RLL": una reinterpretación', in *MLN* 86 (1971), 284–8 (extended in *Eros y Lorca*, 129–52, to include a number of comparable non-*RG* poems); M. Ramond, '"RLL": naissance et signification du thème gitan', in *Imprévue* (Montpellier), no. spécial 1977, 135–67; Andueza, 44–7; McSorley, 82–3; J. B. McInnis and E. E. Bohning, 'The child, the daemon and death in Goethe's "Erlkönig" and GL's "RLL"', in *GLR* 9 (1981), 109–27; Cobb (1983), 63–5; Lisboa, 18–30.

2
PRECIOSA Y EL AIRE

The poem tells of the wind's pursuit of a young gypsy girl and of her narrow escape. The invented myth in Poem 1, said Lorca, was a myth of inland Andalusia, 'Andalucía, interior concentrada y religiosa'; this one is a myth of coastal Andalusia, 'mito de playa tartesa donde el aire es suave como pelusa de melocotón y donde todo drama o danza está sostenido por una aguja inteligente de burla o de ironía' (III, 342). As in 'Romance de la luna, luna' a vulnerable human being is beset by a personified force of nature. Like the moon the anthropomorphic pursuing wind has its origins in popular culture; so has the female object of pursuit.[1] But Preciosa has a more specific and immediate literary source too: Cervantes's Preciosa, the protagonist of his exemplary novel *La gitanilla*:

> Salió la tal Preciosa la más única bailadora que se hallaba en todo el gitanismo, y la más hermosa y discreta que pudiera hallarse, no entre los gitanos, sino entre cuantas hermosas y discretas pudiera pregonar la fama. Ni los soles, ni los aires, ni todas las inclemencias del cielo, a quien más que otras gentes están sujetos los

---

[1] Howard Young cites relevant bibliography (*The Victorious Expression*, 173 n.) and follows Amado Alonso in suggesting the special relevance of the myth of Boreas and Oreithyia as recounted in Ovid's *Metamorphoses* (vi, 675–721). Robert Graves, drawing on earlier, Greek sources (Apollodorus and Apollonius Rhodius), summarises the myth as follows:

> Oreithyia, daughter of Erechtheus, King of Athens, and his wife Praxithea, was one day whirling in a dance beside the river Ilyssus, when Boreas [the North Wind] carried her off to a rock near the river Ergines where, wrapped in a mantle of dark clouds, he ravished her (*The Greek Myths*, Section 48a–b).

See also the four traditional Spanish poems quoted by Rodríguez and Tomlins (in *RoN* 15, 1973–74, 542). I here reproduce two of them:

> No vayas solita al campo
> cuando sople el aire recio;
> porque las niñas son flores
> que hasta las deshoja el viento.

> Un mal ventecillo
> loquillo con mis faldas:
> ¡tira allá, mal viento!
> ¿qué me las alzas?

gitanos, pudieron deslustrar su rostro ni curtir las manos (Cervantes, *OC*, Madrid: Aguilar, 1962, pp. 774–5).

Transposed from a physical to a moral plane the last lines seem especially relevant to the theme of Lorca's poem, and the following passages — all from poems in *La gitanilla* — clearly influenced his imagery and/or syntax:

> Cuando Preciosa el panderete toca,
> y hiere el dulce son los aires vanos (*OC* 787; cf. 1–6);

> La alegría universal,
> huyendo de la congoja,
> calles y plazas discurre,
> descompuesta y casi loca (*OC* 776–7; cf. 5–8);

> san Cristóbal gigante (*OC* 788; cf. 21);

> El dios parlero va en lenguas
> lisonjeras y amorosas (*OC* 776; cf. 22, 42).

What is the significance of these resonances and what is their effect? Lorca, we know, read widely but selectively. With similar selectivity, it seems, he recalled — often unconsciously — lines heard or read, and contemporaries have borne witness to his remarkably retentive memory. But his echoing here of Cervantes's Preciosa was surely conscious, as was his echoing of classical myth. With a more pedestrian artist one might be tempted to think of plagiarism; with Lorca, outstanding for his spontaneously creative imagination, one looks for a more positive explanation. Nor is it difficult to find one. Lorca's Preciosa, if one can imagine her free from resonances, is an ordinary gypsy girl. But because she echoes Cervantes's *gitanilla* she takes on also a wider, representational role. Whereas the plagiarist gains from the reader's ignorance of his sources, Lorca's poetry assumes and gains from the reader's awareness of them. So also with the echoing of the classical story of Boreas and Oreithyia. Preciosa, the gypsy girl, continues as the firm centre and nucleus of Lorca's poem, but wider resonances enhance her stature and significance. We are touching on a basic feature of his writing and on the essence of myth: concentrated significance. In the commentary that follows we shall find further evidence.

1–8. A link with the previous poem has already been suggested by the word *aire* in the title (where *viento* might otherwise seem more appropriate) and the *luna* reappears in the opening image of Preciosa's tambourine as a parchment moon. With its suggestion of whiteness against surrounding darkness the metaphor serves also to prepare us for a night scene (subsequently confirmed in lines 5 and 8) and, by echoing the previous poem, reminds us of the moon as a bewitching dancer, *lúbrica y pura* (cf. 'casta Verónica / del sol', I, 57), thus associating Preciosa too with seductive dancing and cold purity.[2] These associations are reinforced by one's recollection of Cervantes's own *gitanilla*: enticing ('Colgadas del menor de sus cabellos / mil almas lleva', 787) but formidably virtuous ('tan honesta, que en su presencia no osaba alguna gitana vieja ni moza cantar cantares lascivos ni decir palabras no buenas', 775). The path that Lorca's gypsy treads is appropriately amphibious, having both crystal pools (purity again, even glass-like frigidity) and laurel trees (which recall Apollo's pursuit of Daphne).[3] The starless silence, as though in flight from Preciosa's tapping, falls where the sea beats and sings its fish-filled night (a fine image of nature's surging vitality, helped by the four irruptive plosives in *bate y canta*). These opening lines, then, besides presenting a gypsy girl walking along at night and beating her tambourine, also place her, with her seductive art and formidable virtue, on an amphibious path of contrasting elements, amidst a natural world of vitality and fecundity that lies just beyond the exorcising influence of her tambourine. Along the path she treads the laurels anticipate, albeit with only a hint, the main action of the poem: the attempted violation of the girl by an unruly and tempestuous mythical being.

9–16. The description of Preciosa's situation continues, with emphasis now on the more frigid qualities suggested by *cristales*. Whereas lines 7–8 emphasised the sea, down below, with its unbridled vitality, lines 9–12 direct our attention upwards, towards the mountains where *carabineros, guardando, torres, ingleses* — and image-free language

---

[2] Given the poem's classical echoes, it is probably relevant to recall also Artemis (Diana), the moon-goddess and virgin huntress.

[3] Cf. '[Apollo] pursued Daphne, the mountain nymph, a priestess of Mother Earth [...]; but when he overtook her, she cried out to Mother Earth who, in the nick of time, spirited her away to Crete [...]. Mother Earth left a laurel-tree in her place, and from its leaves Apollo made a wreath to console himself' (Graves, *op. cit.*, 21k). For evidence of Lorca's own awareness of this myth see his early 'Invocación al laurel' (1919; I, 135–7).

(except for the humorously deflating paradox in *duermen / guardando*) — suggest order, decorum, repression and confinement. Preciosa's path, then, lies between the two extremes: along the pool-spangled *anfibio sendero*, neither wholly *cristales* nor wholly *laureles*, where in sheer joy the sprite-like gypsies of the water raise up about her arbours of shell-flowers and pine branches, a contrast both to the solid, utilitarian, *carabinero*-protected *blancas torres* of the English above and to the formless, undirected vitality of the night sea below.[4]

17–24. First Preciosa (1–2); then her situation and its ever wider implications (3–16). Though we are scarcely aware of formal divisions as we read, the first sixteen lines are in fact an exposition section, and when the first two lines reappear (17–18) they carry with them resonances that initially they lacked. Then, into Preciosa's world irrupts the wind which, unlike the *carabineros*, never sleeps, a lumbering, naked Saint Christopher, part saint, part Punch-like figure and, ironically in context, the patron saint of travellers. Full of celestial tongues (to entice and seduce, like Cervantes's 'dios parlero', but suggesting also flames of desire) he rises up to watch Preciosa's carefree progress.[5] Lines 23–4 pose a problem. The subject of *tocando*, it is

[4] With the *gitanos del agua* one can perhaps compare the *haditas del agua* of the Generalife, referred to by Lorca in a letter (III, 730). *Caracola* usually means *seashell*, a sea reference that serves to balance the mountain reference implicit in *ramas de pino verde*. Nor is the resonance lost by knowing that in Granada *caracola* refers also to a specific climbing plant (cf. 6:29). The word *sendero*, the contrast between immediate silence (5) and beating sea (7) and the general context suggest that the *anfibio sendero* is not along the beach, as certain critics have suggested, but along the mountain-side, at the mid point between sea and sierra peaks.

[5] In *San Cristobalón* Lorca brings together three traditional elements: (1) the Spanish folklore view of Saint Christopher, traditionally the bearer of Christ, as a hefty, rugged, muscular being; (2) the *cante jondo* tendency to personify the wind as a giant ('lo que en los poemas del cante jondo se acusa como admirable realidad poética es la extraña materialización del viento [...]: aparece como un gigante preocupado de derribar estrellas y disparar nebulosas', III, 209) and (3) the Punch-like puppet Cristóbal ('el puñeterillo don Cristóbal', II, 106), a main character in two of Lorca's plays. The augmentative *Cristobalón* serves to emphasise the paganised saint's lumbering loutishness and is found also in popular tradition (Devoto, in *Filología* II, 1950, 320). As for the *lenguas celestes*, critics may well be correct in seeing them as images of lightning, but the ironic echoing

said, is Saint Christopher who appropriately plays a wind instrument. Grammatically it is possible but not the obvious interpretation. And why *dulce* in view of Saint Christopher's character? And why *ausente*? I am myself inclined to see Preciosa as the subject. She would thus be beating her tambourine and at the same time imitating softly to herself the sound of an accompanying pipe, presumably not the *gaita gallega* *(bagpipe)* but the *gaita* proper, a rustic woodwind instrument much used, together with tabor or tambourine, in popular Spanish *fiestas*.[6] But the combination of pipe and tambourine not only recalls Spanish *fiestas*. It also suggests the bacchanal of classical tradition, much depicted in literature and sculpture. And not only in the literature and sculpture of classical antiquity. Ovid's 'drum of tambourine [...] and the shrill piping of the flute' (*Metamorphoses* iv, 29–30) is echoed in the 'pipes and timbrels' of Keats's celebrated 'Ode on a Grecian Urn', a poem that expresses a poetic ideal close to Lorca's own: art that eternalises, in contrast to sorrowing emotion and transient life. Since Lorca referred enthusiastically to Keats's 'plasticidad admirable' — significantly in his lecture on Góngora's poetic imagery (III, 230; cf. III, 314) — he must surely have known this poem. If he did, further light is thrown on lines 24 and 15–16. The *dulce gaita ausente*, it seems, echoes not so much the 'shrill piping' of Ovid's lines as Keats's 'Heard melodies are sweet, but those unheard [cf. *ausente*] / Are sweeter; therefore, ye soft pipes [cf. *dulce gaita*], play on', and the *glorietas de caracolas / y ramas de pino verde* correspond to Keats's 'happy boughs', 'forest branches' and 'trodden weed'; that is, to the decorative use of vine-boughs, acanthus and the like on a Grecian urn. Lorca, it

of the biblical tongues of fire — and of the 'lenguas lisonjeras y amorosas' of Cervantes's own 'dios parlero' — seems more important, especially in view of lines 25–8, a nice example of the 'delicioso y duro lenguaje' (II, 675) that Lorca associated with Cristóbal and the puppet theatre.

[6] No good case has been made for the traditional interpretation. If one wished to adhere to it — though surely not with *gaita* as bagpipe — one might seek to explain the *dulce gaita* by reference to Ovid's line 'ast ubi blanditiis agitur nil, horridus ira' (685; 'But when he could accomplish nothing by soothing words, rough with anger [etc.]'), but this still leaves problems. Grecian urns, referred to in what follows above, offer no help, for they depict both men and women playing pipes. Lines 35–6, where nature takes up the playing, could conceivably be adduced as evidence in support of my own preferred interpretation.

seems, is here mythicising and stylising Preciosa's adventure into a
Keats-like 'leaf-fring'd legend'.[7]

25–42. Saint Christopher, joyfully paganised into a Dionysian satyr
or Silenus (an aspect of the 'burla o ironía' referred to by Lorca in his
lecture), accosts Preciosa with indecent suggestions that contrast her
youthful purity with his own *dedos antiguos*. The girl flings away her
tambourine — and her moon-like detachment — and takes to her heels
pursued by the big-man wind and his burning sword, an emphatically
male weapon appropriate to the augmentative *Cristobalón* and *viento
hombrón* and a phallic symbol suggesting the heat of desire (in contrast
to the *rosa azul* of the girl's own cold purity). The surrounding world
of nature comes alive to the pursuit. The sea below murmurs its disap-
proval, with an anthropomorphising superposition of sound and sight
(the ripples being seen as a frown), the olives turn pale in horror at
the pursuit and, all around, shade and snow take up Preciosa's earlier
music of invisible pipe (now transposed into *flautas de umbría*) and
white, moon-like tambourine (now *liso gong de la nieve*). As in lines
1–16, the significance of an individual human situation has been enhanced by nature's own response and involvement. At this point the
poet himself intervenes, with admonitions that are also joyous taunts
appropriate to an ostensible gypsy narrator.[8] Line 40 appears fre-

---

[7] I quote further lines from Keats's Ode:

> What men or gods are these? What maidens loth?
> What mad pursuit? What struggle to escape?
> What pipes and timbrels? What wild ecstasy?

Since Lorca had little or no knowledge of English he must have depended
on a translation: either into Spanish (though I know of no Spanish translation prior to 28 January 1926, the date of Lorca's only known manuscript
of 'Preciosa y el aire') or into French (John Keats, *Poèmes et poésies*, trans.
Paul Gallimard, Paris 1910). Given the similarity between the French
translator's introductory reference to Keats's 'effet de plastique insurpas-
sable' (p. 23) and Lorca's own reference to Keats's 'plasticidad admirable'
(III, 230) it seems at least probable that Lorca knew the French translation.
One is tempted also to find in the French rendering of Keats's 'Fair youth'
(line 15) as 'Bel éphèbe' a possible source for Lorca's description of Saint
Michael as *efebo de tres mil noches* (8:26).

[8] *Or the randy old wind will catch you* (cf. *un viejo verde, a lustful old
man, dirty old man*). The association of green with nature is relevant too.

quently in songs associated with Holy Week (cf. Lorca's own 'Saeta', I, 184) but in the present context the words herald no submissive Christ-like figure. It is part of the narrator's taunt (more 'burla o ironía') and a further invitation to the reader to find, beneath the echoes of Christian saint and Holy Week, the surging of more primitive, pagan forces. As earlier lines suggested and as line 41 now confirms, the Saint Christopher from whom Preciosa seeks escape is a satyr, the traditional terror of classical nymphs. The Holy Ghost's 'cloven tongues like as of fire' (Acts 2:3) are burning tongues of sexual desire (42).

43–58. Preciosa has escaped in terror from the realm of shade, across the snow, to the refuge of white towers, English consul and officially (even officiously) dressed *carabineros*. It is a prosaic world, utterly foreign to her, and Lorca's humorously deflating duality *asustados/carabineros* recalls his corresponding earlier duality *duermen/guardando*. The language, too, is notably prosy and image-free, in contrast to the rich imagery used in the presentation of natural elements.[9] Though the virtuous Preciosa apparently drinks the lukewarm milk she is offered, she does not drink the Englishman's gin. Perhaps she sees this as another, more sophisticated and 'civilised' attempt on her honour.[10] As at the beginning of the poem, with the *anfibio sendero / de cristales y laureles*, — and as elsewhere in *Romancero gitano*, most notably the Antoñito poems (nos. 11 and 12) — Lorca is pointing to the difficulty

[9] Díaz-Plaja, in his brief commentary on this poem, emphasises 'el uso de *un lenguaje lleno de audacia metafórica conviviendo con un lenguaje extremadamente normal*' (D-P's italics) and suggests it is typical of the whole book. But he appears to have overlooked the fact that in each of the examples he quotes of *audacia metafórica* Lorca is evoking nature and that in each of the quoted examples of *lenguaje extremadamente normal* ('prosa simple, popular', 'llana prosa rimada') he is describing the archetypally prosaic English consul and his carabineer guards. We shall find a similar duality in poems where civil guards appear. To write prosily is at times a sign of poetic genius. It is also, in Lorca's case, a pointer to his dramatic sensitivity. Critical disregard of this dramatic sensitivity accounts, I believe, for the misinterpretation of several poems in *Romancero gitano*.

[10] After describing his aims in 'Preciosa y el aire' to his friend and fellow poet Jorge Guillén, Lorca continued: 'Quedará un libro de romances y se podrá decir que es un libro de Andalucía. ¡Eso sí! Andalucía no me vuelve la espalda ..., yo sé que ella no se ha acostado con ningún inglés' (III, 884).

of the middle way. The unpleasantness of the extremes reappears in the final lines as Preciosa, in tears, tells her story to *aquella gente* (a dismissive and disdainful expression) while the wind, in his frustrated desire, bites angrily at the slates on the roof.

Published commentaries are generally in line with the above, though much is overlooked. Aside from consensus, Feal Deibe and Allen both subject the poem to depth psychology but arrive, perhaps surprisingly, at different interpretations. Feal Deibe's approach was illustrated in the commentary on Poem 1 and I here confine myself to Allen's. Basically, he believes, the poem is concerned with 'a breach of continuity in the ego-structure of the protagonist'. Given the length of his commentary and its dense erudition I am obliged to illustrate rather than summarise. His three-page interpretation of lines 3–4 is basic to his case and is appropriately summed up by the author himself:

> We have tried to show, how the laurel is intimately bound up with the phenomenon of life rooted in the land masses and so launched on the evolutionary journey culminating in the appearance of ego-consciousness — a rechanneling or 'sublimation' of the vital impulse towards noninstinctual ends; a conversion of libidinal heat into libidinal light. In *Preciosa and the Wind* the 'crystals' of the sea (the result of tidal motion illuminated by the moon) reveal only the presence of a vague and undifferentiated surge; whereas the laurels on the other side of the 'amphibious' threshold represent the differentiated growth of land-rooted forms harking back to the abrogation of the purely lascivious impulse of the enamored Sun God.

It is not certain that one's understanding and appreciation of the poem is much enhanced by this. Besides, Allen's interpretation rests rather heavily on the questionable assumption that Preciosa is walking along the seashore, 'specifically the intertidal zone'. Without that seashore the alleged interplay between 'great womb' ('undifferentiated surge') and 'stable land realm' ('the evolutionary journey') seems to be somewhat undermined. It is not the only point in Allen's study where a heavy structure rests on uncertain foundations.

Select bibliography: Díaz-Plaja, 116–18; Correa, 26–8; Henry, 222–3; Nims, 232–6; O. Frattoni, *La forma en Góngora, y otros ensayos*, Rosario 1961, 23–34; J. C. Forster, 'Aspects of Lorca's Saint Christopher', in *BHS* 43 (1966), 109–16; D. Bary, 'Preciosa and the

English', in *HR* 37 (1969), 510–17; R. C. Allen, *The Symbolic World of FGL*, Albuquerque 1972, 11–33, 189–91; Feal Deibe, 153–74; McSorley, 83–4; Cobb (1983), 65–8; Lisboa, 32–45; D. Harris, 'El *RG* o el baile de burlas y veras', in *Las Nuevas Letras* (Almeria), no. 2 (Spring 1985), 47–51.

3
REYERTA

Gypsy quarrels and fights, usually between members of rival families, are commonplace in Andalusia and are much reported in the popular press. Lorca's change of title, from the earlier 'Reyerta de mozos' and 'Reyerta de gitanos', served to reduce this anecdotic, local-colour element and parallels the change of title in Poem 1.[1] Besides, the word *mozos* especially lacks tragic overtones. By eliminating it Lorca placed maximum emphasis on the *reyerta* itself. It would be going too far to say that the *reyerta* has thereby become a threatening force akin to the moon and the wind in the preceding poems, but by removing the *mozos* Lorca has at least opened the way to this possibility. The title 'Reyerta' is potentially more mythical and more tragic than 'Reyerta de mozos'. It also prepares us better for what Lorca himself said he had expressed in the poem: 'esa lucha sorda latente en Andalucía y en toda España de grupos que se atacan sin saber por qué, por causas misteriosas, por una mirada, por una rosa, porque un hombre de pronto siente un insecto sobre la mejilla, por un amor de hace dos siglos' (III, 343).

1–4. First, specific placing that echoes ballad and other popular literature ('Por aquel postigo viejo ...'; 'En los campos de Alventosa ...'); then emphasis on the instruments of death (elevated in significance by association with Albacete, the traditional centre of Spanish knife manufacture); next, an evocation of the dual bloodshed (with almost festive gloating); finally, another physical image to suggest the darting and flashing of the knives. The lines confirm, in part at least, one's feeling about the changed title. The emphasis is not on anecdotic protagonists but on the fight itself at its very centre. For the rest one notes how, as at the beginning of Poems 10 and 11, there is a

[1] 'Reyerta de mozos': autograph version, 9 September 1926 (III, 895–6); published version, in *La Verdad, Suplemento Literario* (Murcia) 59, 10 October 1926; 'Reyerta de gitanos', in *L'Amic de les Arts* (Sitges) 15, 30 June 1927, p. 45.

progressive build-up of significant elements — and thus also of tension —, with a *cante*-like release in the final line.

5–8. The harsh playing-card light has suggested to some commentators conflict over a game of cards. It could well be so, though I myself find this reading too anecdotic and difficult to reconcile with Lorca's own words quoted above. More relevant perhaps is the combination of *naipe, caballo* and *jinete*, for the eleventh card in the Spanish pack depicts a horse and rider. Moreover, in a gypsy context especially cards are associated with fortune-telling. *Dura* in *dura luz de naipe* would thus suggest not only the physical harshness of light but also the relentlessness of fate, further reflected in nature's own *agrio verde*. It is another example, then, both of Lorca's visual sensitivity and of his tendency to find wider resonances in sense perceptions. There is a further example in the juxtaposition of *caballos enfurecidos* and *perfiles de jinetes*. As in Poem 1 (25–8) firm profile suggests the proud, fully aware human being (cf. also 'Busca su perfil seguro, / y el sueño lo desorienta', I, 554). But in the heat of the fight the riders' 'perfil seguro' is threatened and their fury is appropriately transferred to the horses which, like playing cards, are associated by Lorca with the threat of death. We shall find the same key elements in another *RG* poem of heralded misfortune, 'Romance del emplazado' (Poem 14): *naipes helados* (frozen hard in what they foretell), 'bitter' torment (epitomised in the protagonist's name, Amargo), the horse that expresses its rider's emotive state, and the proud *perfil*, there finally attained in the stoic response to death.

9–12. The tragic dimension of the conflict is further emphasised by the weeping of two old women, presumably mothers (cf. the Madre in *Bodas de sangre*). Their 'suspensión irreal en la copa de un árbol' has suggested to Josephs and Caballero certain of Goya's 'black' paintings (233). But there is a considerable stylistic difference between Goya and Lorca, and the nearest comparable Goya painting depicts four witch-like fates floating in the air rather than two women in a tree. Figures in trees are found, however, in fifteenth-century paintings and illuminations and I am inclined to see lines 9–10 as an example of Lorca's neo-primitivism and, more especially, of his much neglected debt to late medieval and early Renaissance art.[2] There is a further example in the following two lines where the poet gives physical form to a popular expression (*subirse por las paredes, to go off at the deep*

end, climb up the wall [in anger or exasperation]) and shows a mythical
bull of strife, the epitome of animal power, as he actually clambers up
walls, like a bull climbing the *barrera* of a bullring. It is just the sort of
thing that Bruegel did in the sixteenth century in painting, with the
literal representation of expressions such as *armed to the teeth, falling
between two stools, running one's head against a brick wall, speaking
with two mouths* and a hundred or so more.[3]

13-16. Lorca's primitivism continues: first in his evocation of angels
bearing kerchiefs and snow water (to staunch blood and cool wounds;
cf. II, 948); then in the image of their wings as Albacete knives, for
the classical Albacete *navaja* blade has a sweeping, tapered shape not
unlike the stylised folded wings represented in early paintings. But this
image of the angels' wings also introduces a darker note, for it recalls
line 2 and thus associates the angels more closely with the fight itself.
Perhaps they are not merely ministering angels, then. Perhaps they are

[2] Rafael Alberti offers a nice pointer to Lorca's delight in primitive
imagery (including that of a figure in an olive tree) in his description of
their first meeting, when Alberti himself was still still known principally as
a painter:

> Me dijo, entre otras cosas, haber visto, años atrás, mi exposición del
> Ateneo; que yo era su primo y que deseaba encargarme un cuadro
> en el que se le viera dormido a orillas de un arroyo y arriba, allá en lo
> alto de un olivo, la imagen de la Virgen, ondeando en una cinta [another
> pointer to early painting] la siguiente leyenda: 'Aparición de Nuestra
> Señora del Amor Hermoso al poeta Federico García Lorca' (*La arboleda
> perdida*, Buenos Aires 1959, p. 172).

Romance influence too may be relevant. I quote from the 'Romance de
la Infantina', translated by J. G. Lockhart under the title 'The Lady of the
Tree':

> En una rama más alta,
> viera estar una infantina;
> cabellos de su cabeza
> todo el roble cobrían.

(*Romances viejos castellanos*, ed. Wolf, Hofmann, Menéndez y Pelayo,
Madrid 1928, I, 267; hereafter *RVC*).
The ability to respond to the naïve magic of such images is a basic
requirement for the enjoyment of *Romancero gitano*.
[3] On this and the pre-Bruegel tradition of such painting see Walter S.
Gibson, *Bruegel*, London 1977, pp. 65-79.

in touch with dark forces that prompt and guide such fights. They are, after all, black angels. Something else points in the same direction. After a succession of present tenses the angels' appearance is heralded by a switch to the imperfect *traían*. This makes it clear, as the present tense would not, that the bringing of *pañuelos* is not simply the next thing that happens. *Traían* suggests that the act of bringing is progressive and that it was already taking place during the action of the previous lines, perhaps even as far back as the parallel line 2. The black angels, then, do not simply appear and then disappear. Their activity spreads out beyond the lines in which they are explicitly mentioned. So does their impact. We shall find further evidence.

17-22. Juan Antonio el de Montilla (a superbly resonant name) rolls dead down the slope, his body full of *lirios* (an image of knife wounds) and a *granada* (indicating a contused wound) on his temple.[4] But the images are not only physical. Like the chrysanthemum the *lirio* is a traditional flower of death, and the *granada*, a traditional symbol of life (developed elsewhere by Lorca as 'corazón que late', 'sangre', 'luz de la vida', 'pasión', I, 105-7), since it is *en las sienes*, here represents a visible loss of life (cf. *Bodas de sangre*, with *sangre* as both life and, when spilt, as death). Adequate translation into English is impossible. *Lirios* can be accurately, though not pleasantly, rendered as *irises*, but *lilies*, which sounds better, are *azucenas* and, being the flower of the Annunciation (and thus of purity), they would here have an inappropriate emotive association. Similarly, *granada*, as a symbol of life (frequent in early paintings) can be adequately, though not pleasantly, rendered as *pomegranate* but the Spanish word also has resonances of the destruction of life (*grenade*), a duality that is relevant to the poem but impossible to convey in English. But whatever the limitations of translation, the stylising primitivism of *lirios* and *granadas* for wounds is obvious and is further emphasised by the words' traditional

---

[4] This use of *granada* is common in Andalusian speech, though not in Castilian: *El niño se ha hecho un chichón / una granada (un chichón* for a bump, lump or 'egg'; *una granada* when the bump is broken and bleeding). A popular song of the 1920s and/or 1930s tells of the unhappy love of a singer, La Lirio, and includes lines relevant to Lorca's, with a similar use of the *lirio*'s purple colour as an image of suffering:

> La Lirio, la Lirio tiene
> tiene una pena la Lirio
> que se le han puesto las sienes
> moraítas como el lirio.

resonances. The impact on the reader, as with the earlier knives, *bellas de sangre contraria*, and as with much fifteenth-century painting, is a strange mixture of vividness and detachment. It is a good example of Lorca's conscious escape both from the diffuse contours of Romantic poetry and from the Romantic's demand of total emotional involve-ment. The stylising primitivism continues yet further in his final image of the dead Juan Antonio, *perfil*-proud to the last, riding off to death on a cross of fire.

23–30. The change of tone is abrupt and akin to the appearance of *carabineros* and *ingleses* in the previous poem. But there is a fine superposition of images (personification, transferred epithet [hypall-age], metaphor and onomatopoeia) to evoke the slithered blood that moans its muted serpent song.[5] Then back to prosaic officialdom with its dismissive attitude to what has occurred and the final ironic refer-ence to the deaths of Romans and Carthaginians. Their wars for the possession of Spain are well known. What the magistrate here means, then, is that it is the same old story: age-old rivalries and conflicts resulting in death.[6] The increased number (for only one death has been indicated) suggests detached unconcern prompted by long experience of such events.

31–8. But though the magistrate is detached and unconcerned, nature is not, and the afternoon, with its vitality of bristling fig-trees and hot murmurs, swoons on the horsemen's wounded thighs (com-pare the transfer of anger from horsemen to horses in lines 7–8). Meanwhile, black angels were flying across the western sky. It has been suggested that they are clouds and it is possible to assume that this is the real-life justification for the image. But there is no need for such justification, any more than there is with the black angels that hover over the cross in Rogier van der Weyden's famous Vienna Crucifixion. Lorca's angels, I suggest, are similarly visionary and unfettered by

[5] For an extensive commentary on lines 25–6, see Pedro Laín Entralgo, *La aventura de leer*, Madrid 1956, pp.162–8 ('García Lorca, o la intuición sensorial de la realidad' [1952]).

[6] Barea has urged the relevance of 'los disfraces tradicionales de las procesiones religiosas de Andalucía, judíos, romanos, cartagineses, con sus trajes fantásticos y anacrónicos' (*El poeta y su pueblo*, Buenos Aires 1956, p. 21); Molina Fajardo has recalled that 'en un colegio de Granada se solía dividir a los alumnos para competencias de tipo escolar en romanos y cartagineses' (Josephs and Caballero, 234).

physical reality. Other things are in any case more important. What has been said of *traían* in line 13 can now be said also of *volaban* in line 35: because of the imperfect tense the activity spreads out beyond the lines in which it is explicitly mentioned. Indeed, given the similar effect of the imperfects in lines 13 and 35 and the parallel lines 2 and 16, the presence of the black angels seems to underlie all the other actions presented and ultimately to infuse the whole poem — one of the few daylight poems in *Romancero gitano* — with an overall impression of darkness that the various indications of light (4, 5, 21) seem to enhance rather than diminish. The *largas trenzas* and *corazones de aceite* of the final lines confirm what one has perhaps suspected. That these are specifically gypsy angels. But being black angels they appear also as angels of ill omen and dark fate. Are they perhaps a gypsy echo of the winged classical harpies, 'souls of the dead [that] snatch away those of the living'?[7] And do they fulfil their function through the *reyerta*, as angels of discord? If so, *reyertas* between men, 'sin saber por qué, por causas misteriosas', are ultimately *reyertas* between men and their black angels with wings of Albacete knives, and other men are merely instruments of the angels' will. The black angels would thus be akin to the moon for the child (Poem 1) and the wind for Preciosa (Poem 2): dark powers that beset the gypsies with further causes for black sorrow. While nature responds to the agony of the wounded, the angels themselves, their task accomplished — a further indication that they are not mere ministering angels —, fly away across the western sky.

Unlike the previous poems 'Reyerta' has been poorly served by critics and studies are generally lightweight. In one of the only two substantial commentaries Feal Deibe, as in Poems 1 and 2, proposes a Freudian reading, starting from the interpretation of the *barranco* (1) as a womb symbol. To the present writer at least his findings are unconvincing. Lisboa's reading is soundly text-based.

Select bibliography: Campbell, 44; Correa, 28–9; Feal Deibe, 175–88; D. K. Loughran, 'Imagery of nature and its function in Lorca's poetic drama: "Reyerta" and *Bodas de sangre*', in *The World of Nature* ..., ed. J. W. Zdenek, 1980, 55–61; Cobb (1983), 68–9; Lisboa, 47–53.

[7] *The Oxford Companion to Classical Literature*, ed. Paul Harvey, Oxford 1940, p. 194.

4
ROMANCE SONÁMBULO

Though one of the earliest of Lorca's *romances gitanos* to be written —
along with *RG* 7 and 17 —, 'Romance sonámbulo' did not appear in
print prior to its publication in *Romancero gitano* in July 1928. For
many readers it is the finest poem in the book; for Rafael Alberti it was
the greatest *romance* in modern Spanish literature. It is also the poem
that has been most variously and extensively commented on. And yet,
despite a number of sensitive studies, several aspects of the poem
appear to have been overlooked or underemphasised, most notably
the interplay of illusion and disillusion that runs through the poem
and concludes with the virtual victory of the latter. It is perhaps an
indication of how a great poem can work its magic without the reader's
being intellectually aware of the elements that produce that magic.

At her railing — possibly a balcony railing; more probably the railing
of a typical Andalusian *azotea* (flat, terrace roof) — a girl awaits the
return of her lover, apparently away on a smuggling expedition. The
lover arrives badly wounded, goes up with the girl's father to where
the girl was earlier waiting and finds her dead. Civil guards come to
arrest him. This, it seems, is the underlying anecdote and is generally
accepted as such by critics. But the evidence consists of mere suggestions: the boat, the horse, the anxious waiting, the Andalusian and
gypsy context, the wounded lover, an apparent fight in the mountain
passes, the father's distraught response, the arrival of civil guards and,
from outside the poem, the Spanish system (until the 1950s) of both
national and internal customs barriers, the smuggling tradition that was
still very much alive in the first quarter of the twentieth century and
Lorca's own indication of the presence somewhere in *Romancero
gitano* (though he does not where) of 'la nota vulgar del contraban-
dista' (III, 340). But mere narrative plays little part in the poem and
nothing *vulgar* remains. Pointers to a smuggling expedition are
glimpsed only momentarily amidst a succession of dreamlike images.
The finished work of art is a characteristically Lorcan 'sleepwalking
ballad' of yearning and lamentation.

1–12. The yearning appears immediately in the superbly magical, incantatory opening lines. The first line was apparently taken from the opening of a popular *romance*: 'Verde que te quiero verde / de color de aceituna' (Cobb, 1983). But whereas the range of *verde* in the traditional poem is immediately restricted by *de color de aceituna* (to suggest an Andalusian girl's olive complexion) Lorca's green takes on wider and less contoured resonances and these radiate increasingly as the poem progresses. In line 2, for example, *verde* suggests not only expansive colour (with no restrictive articles) but also freshness, freedom and life. It is this that the poet longs for, with everything in its natural place (3–4).[1] But the appearance of the girl in the following lines denies his longing with suggestions of withdrawal from life (*sombra; sueña; ojos de fría plata*), and *verde* here is no longer the colour of freshness but the colour of putrefaction (*verde carne, pelo verde*).[2] Now the repeated opening line is more forlorn (9). The clamour for green as life is threatened by contradictory resonances of green as death. Under the gypsy moon, the physical cause of the colour *verde* in line 7 but also, more importantly, the malevolent source of the accompanying death associations (cf. the death-bringing moon of primitive cultures referred to above, Poem 1), objects seem more alive than the girl herself.

13–24. Again the poet affirms his longing for green, and again his longing is denied, this time by the surrounding world of nature. For the coming dawn is not green. Instead it appears in shimmers of cold

---

[1] Cf. Bendita sea por siempre
la Santísima Trinidad,
y guarde al hombre en la sierra
y al marinero en el mar (*Mariana Pineda*; II, 205).

On the first line see also Francisco García Lorca, 'Verde', in *Homenaje a Casalduero: crítica y poesía*, ed. Rizel Pincus Sigele and Gonzalo Sobejano, Madrid 1972, pp. 135–9.

[2] Cf. 'Era una carne verdosa y de muerte' (III, 82); 'gigantes cabezas / [...] con órbitas vacías / y verdosas cabelleras' (I, 18). With the colour green as elsewhere Lorca exploits expressive potentials inherent in everyday language: 'green grass' suggests fresh grass (pleasant); 'green almonds' suggests bitter almonds (unpleasant). Lorca's sensitivity to sense perceptions is well known. His sensitivity to the shifting meaning of words in context is equally notable but less recognised.

white against the surrounding darkness (*estrellas de escarcha; pez de sombra*). And the fig-tree, with a suggestion of dryness rather than freshness, rubs its tamed wind (not the fresh, free *verde viento*) with the sandpaper of its branches (very different from the longed-for *verdes ramas*).[3] And the mountain, as though aware of a threatening presence, bristles up its pointed agaves (harsh cactus plants) like a cat caught filching (an image prompted, perhaps, by *frota su viento*, as if the wind were a dog). The sense imagery prompts correspondingly unpleasant emotive responses: the cold, fish-like clamminess and half light of the approaching dawn (sight and touch), the harshness of the branches (sound) and the ominous agaves on the mountain top as they become visible against the dawning sky (sight). The catlike bristling of the agaves suggested someone's approach and this is taken up in the questions of the following line (21). But we are given no answers. Even in this, life is unresponsive. Instead, there is insistence again on the girl's deathly green and on her dreaming, presented now, in harmony with the inhospitable world around, as a dream of life's bitter disillusion, with the echoing of a well-known and much glossed traditional poem of unhappy love: 'Miraba la mar / la mal casada, / que miraba la mar / cómo es ancha y larga'.[4] The similarity between lines 5–7 and 22–4 should not be missed. There are four main elements in common — the girl (6, 22), the railing (6, 22), the ominous green of flesh and hair (7, 23) and the dreaming (6, 24) — and two that might appear to be different: *la sombra en la cintura* (5) and *la mar amarga* (24). But the common elements oblige us to draw these apparently different elements together. The shadow at the girl's waist was not merely the

---

[3] Lines 17–20 are among the most quoted and commented lines in *Romancero gitano*, usually out of context and always without adequate consideration of context. I know of no critic, for example, who notes the tacit rejection of the poet's longing (9) that is offered by the manifest absence of green. One recent commentater even refers to the 'ruido que producen las hojas al moverse con el viento, para hacer que las hojas limen el aire' and later returns to the point: '[la higuera] cuyas hojas liman el viento, el viento que hace que se ericen las pitas como pelo de gato amenazado'. But the main point of the image is surely that the poet's longed-for green is absent. Nature responds to the poet's yearning for green freshness and life with coldness, whiteness and rasping dryness — all epitomised in the absence of leaves.

[4] Dámaso Alonso and José M. Blecua, *Antología de la poesía española (Poesía de tipo tradicional)*, Madrid 1956, pp. 85, 232.

physical moon-cast shadow of the railing but also the shade of disillusion that was gradually engulfing her, and *soñar en* means not only
dreaming of the bitter sea but also *dreaming (engulfed) in* the bitter sea
(of life and destiny).

25–52. The scene changes. Two men, apparently the girl's father and
her lover, are talking together. The younger man has arrived badly
wounded from the passes of Cabra (with characteristic stylisation of his
wounds) and wants to exchange horse, saddle and knife (the single
man's life of adventure) for house, mirror and blanket (domesticity).
The older man would accept the change, he says, but his fortunes are
upturned. Why? Does he wish merely to dissociate himself from a man
pursued by the Civil Guard? Or does he fear ruin because of his own
involvement in the smuggling (since the guards know where to come,
81–2)? Or is he distracted by awareness of his daughter's imminent
death? Appropriately in a sleepwalking ballad it is not clear. Here as
elsewhere in the poem there is, in Lorca's words, 'una gran sensación
de anécdota, un agudo ambiente dramático' (III, 341), but causes and
events are shrouded in mystery. In the world of *Romancero gitano* —
and of its author — the fates press constantly upon man, without any
easy, logical explanation, their relentless 'no puede ser'. In the present
case we feel this not only because of these lines but also because lines
1–12 and 13–24 have prepared us for the same duality: on the one
hand what is longed for; on the other what life offers. Again the young
man expresses his longing — now merely to die decently in a steel bed
of his own with cambric sheets (a great illusion for this gypsy who
perhaps sleeps usually on horse or floor) — but again it is rejected.[5]
Still further longing is expressed in lines 47–50, with the triple
appearance of *dejadme* which broadens the earlier singular *ves* (39) and
involves the reader too in his clamour,[6] and the *altas barandas* and

---

[5] The following *bulería*, which I have transcribed from oral tradition,
expresses a related sentiment (though the *techao* here refers presumably to
the coffin lid and the earth that covers it):

> Mira si soy desgraciao, (bis)
> que tengo que esperar a morirme
> para dormir bajo techao.

[6] A number of recent editions have *veis* in line 39 (as Lorca did in his
non-definitive 1924 manuscript, I, 1147) to bring it into line with 47 and 49.
But all *RG* editions published in Lorca's lifetime have *ves*, which I find

verdes barandas recall the *baranda* where the girl was submerged in shade. But now the *barandas* are less material. They suggest a yearning for ultimate illusion as the moment of death approaches,[7] and this yearning is emphasised again in lines 50–1 through the sheer intoxication of sound- and word-play: *hasta las verdes barandas. / Barandales de la luna (up to the high railings. / Handrails of the moon).* Both by its climactic placing and by its sound the word *barandales* offers an emotive intensification (a sort of superlative) of the preceding *barandas* and serves as an appropriate transition to the fatal realm of the moon. But *barandales de la luna* suggest also foaming moonlit rivers and this brings us back to the real-life natural context. It is almost imagery for the sheer joy of imagery. But not quite, for the rivers of Lorca's moon, the gypsy moon, remind us of the sea of death (the *mar amarga*) into which they flow.

53–60. The young man's last entreaty is not rejected and the two go up towards the high railings where the girl was waiting. It is a procession of suffering, but stylised, as in the incantatory lines 55–6, and the glints of dawn themselves appear both as elements in a procession (*farolillos de hojalata; mil panderos de cristal*) and as pointers to the agony involved (*temblaban; herían*).

61–72. The repeated first two lines of the poem now echo rather forlornly amidst the general context of disillusion and suffering, and the switch to the preterite, *subieron*, besides indicating a time lapse, suggests only a muted fulfilment of the action indicated in lines 53–4, with no evidence of attained *altas barandas*. On the contrary, there is

grammatically more usual and stylistically more effective. In lines 67–8 the young man, again specifically addressing his *compadre*, naturally returns to the singular form.

[7] *Mariana Pineda* again offers a notable parallel. The protagonist has been condemned to death after separation from her lover, but will hopefully be reunited with him 'en las altas barandas' (II, 272). Compare also the opening lines of the traditional 'Romance de Santa Catalina': 'Por la baranda del cielo / se pasea una zagala, / vestida de azul y blanco, / que Catalina se llama' (*RVC* III, 199), and, as in Lorca's poem, the association of *barandas* and moon noted by Aguirre in the following 'adivinanza': 'Por las barandas del cielo / se pasea una doncella / vestida de azul y blanco / y reluce como una estrella', to which the answer is 'La luna' (*BHS* 53, 1976, 127).

bitterness in the strange pungent taste of the wind, and the wind is not green but a long wind that suggests the painful, fruitless quest. The brief dialogue confirms the point. Where is your *niña amarga* (with an echo of the earlier *mar amarga*)? The only reply is a recollection of how she was formerly, with fresh face and black hair, before the moon enveloped her in green and shade. One observes again, in lines 69–70, the magical, incantatory use of language to express yearning.

73–86. There is another scene change and a characteristically Lorcan use of the imperfect tense (74) to indicate action already in progress, in this case singularly passive action more akin to a descriptive state. The impression in context is of destiny fulfilled. In harmony with the poem's train of disillusion, the girl now floats, dead and green, on the surface of the storage tank as though held up by an icicle of moonbeam. The narrative basis becomes clearer. Bewitched by the *luna gitana* and already half engulfed in shade at the beginning of the poem, she has finally been lured by the moon and its reflection in the *aljibe* and cast herself, like a sleepwalker, into the water. It is the immediate nucleus justification for the poem's title and it obliges us to mute critics' frequent references to suicide. The night has become intimate as though in sympathy. It is a fine example of Lorca's expressionistic use of context. The dawn has appeared, but the harsh dawn could never be intimate. We return, then, to the emotively more appropriate darkness of night. It is akin to the use of so-called arbitrary colour in painting. But now drunken civil guards are beating on the door. Drunk to give them courage perhaps, or drunk because they themselves have been sampling captured brandy (cf. Poem 11).[8] But drunk especially because of the scorn the narrator feels for them at their irruption into this painful moment of intimacy (emotive justification again). The poem ends with the fullest restatement yet of the opening of the poem. But the meaning now is different. At the beginning the same four lines expressed a yearning for greenness and freshness and life. Now, at the end of the poem, new depths have been revealed. Green is not only the colour of freshness; it is also the colour of moon-induced (that is, fate-guided) putrefaction. One looks for life in its happiness and one finds life in its despair — like the girl, like her father, like her lover. The last

---

[8] There is a weakness in the latter suggestion. So far as I know, smugglers in Andalusia were involved principally with coffee and tobacco, not alcohol.

four lines present a superposition of the two planes: on the one hand,
life and longing; on the other, disillusion and death. Under life's
happier appearances lies constantly, for Lorca, its inevitable tragedy:
'bajo la acacia en flor / del jardín, mi muerte acecha' (*Mariana Pineda*,
II, 253).

Among the commentaries listed below (and many others that I have
been obliged to omit) there are notable differences of interpretation
from my own. Barea, Allen and András, for example, all emphasise
the underlying narrative, interpreting it in different ways: Barea with
an imaginative reconstruction of the consensus smuggling expedition;
Allen with a tale of marital infidelity involving the girl, her lover
(wounded by the husband) and the husband himself (who has killed
his wife, thrown her body into the storage tank and now, in insane
revenge, shows her lover the corpse); András with a story of civil
guards who have forced their attentions on the girl during the lover's
absence and now, in drunken revelry, come in search of further sexual
favours. Closer to the poem itself Nims, Aguirre, Allen, Cárdenas and
McSorley believe that the girl is already dead when the poem opens;
Cobb, Aguirre, Havard and Semprún Donahue purport to find evidence of homosexuality; Gicovate looks for clearer understanding by
changing Lorca's punctuation, on occasion against the evidence of
how Lorca himself read the poem (cf. Guillén in FGL, *OC* I, xlviii);
András, still with emphasis on narrative progression and neglect of the
poem's magical sleepwalking qualities, suggests the passage of a day
between the coming of dawn (57–60) and the reappearance of night
(79–80); also, understandably in view of his above indicated interpretation of the underlying narrative, he finds pointers to a social message.
In the most recent commentary known to me Miller finds a Jungian
archetypal drama:

> The entire dramatic action takes place in the imagination [of the
> wounded gypsy] during the final minutes of his life. What appear
> to be two supporting characters, a young woman and her father,
> are actually the archetypal projections of the *Anima* figure and the
> Wise Old Man, who are unconsciously evoked by the Gypsy in an
> attempt to find a way to retain his hold on life and to reorient
> himself towards a better, more harmonious balance between
> unconscious and conscious mental functioning.

Finally, *verde*, even in lines 1–2, is interpreted in very different ways,
ranging from life (the consensus), through homosexuality (Semprún

Donahue) to death (Cárdenas). Despite frequent references to the limited importance of narrative in this poem and to the supremacy of its imagery, I know of no study that shows the interaction of images throughout the poem and thereby demonstrates the struggle between illusion and disillusion with which Lorca here replaces traditional narrative. It is this gap especially that I have sought to fill in my own commentary.

Select bibliography: Barea, *El poeta y su pueblo* [1944], Buenos Aires 1956, 128–32; P. Darmangeat, 'Essai d'interprétation de "RS"', in *LNL* 136 (1956), 1–11; Correa, 29–33; B. Gicovate, 'El "RS" de GL', in *Hispania* 41 (1958), 300–2; Henry, 223–6; Nims, 237–42; J. M. Aguirre, 'El sonambulismo de FGL', in *BHS* 44 (1967), 267–85; Cobb (1967), 65–8; R. Allen, 'An analysis of narrative and symbol in Lorca's "RS"', in *HR* 36 (1968), 338–52; J. Velasco, 'A la découverte du *RG* de FGL: "RS"', in *LNL* 188–9 (1969), 53–67; B. J. DeLong-Tonelli, 'The lyric dimension in Lorca's "RS"', in *RoN* 12 (1970–71), 289–95; R. G. Havard, 'The symbolic ambivalence of 'green' in GL and Dylan Thomas', in *MLR* 67 (1972), 810–19; D. L. Cárdenas, 'Otra interpretación de "RS"', in *ETL* 1 (1972–73), 111–18; M. de Semprún Donahue, 'Nuevos indicios en la interpretación de "RS"', in *CA* 33, 3 (May-June 1974), 257–60; L. András, 'El caso de la gitana sonámbula', in *Actas del Simposio Internacional de Estudios Hispánicos* [1976], Budapest 1978, 181–94; Andueza, 48–65; T. A. Pabón, 'El ciclo vida-muerte en el "RS" de FGL', in *Arbor* 101 (September-December 1978), 249–55; McSorley, 81–9; G. Salvador, *Glosas al 'RS' de GL*, Granada 1980; Cobb (1983), 69–73; Lisboa, 56–70; N. C. Miller, '"RS", an archetypal drama', in *HJ* 7, 2 (Spring 1986), 17–24.

5
LA MONJA GITANA

The poem exists in a single manuscript, with much reworking that does not, however, make the version definitive ('20 de Agosto 1925'; *A* I, 142–5). Like 'Romance sonámbulo' it was first published in 1928 in *Romancero gitano*.

'The *Gipsy Nun*', writes Roy Campbell, 'is a very pleasant piece of verbal embroidery' (*Lorca*, 48). In fact it is rather more than that, and in the threads of his embroidery Lorca dramatises his most recurrent theme, that of vitality and its repression. This is immediately akin to the interplay of illusion and disillusion in the previous poem and the title itself epitomises the conflict: on the one hand the protagonist is a gypsy — freedom, vitality, *gracia*, fantasy —; on the other hand she is a nun — confinement, discipline, menial tasks. She is an extreme example, then, of something that concerned Lorca from an early date. In vain do men shut themselves away in monasteries, he wrote in his teenage *Impresiones y paisajes* (1918); 'el alma sigue apasionada, y estos hombres buenos, infelices, que buscan a Dios en estos desiertos del dolor, debían comprender que eran inútiles las torturas de la carne cuando el espíritu pide otra cosa' (III, 25). Similarly with women: 'Las monjas, en su debilidad infantil, se encerraron en el convento, tapándose el camino del olvidar .... Lo que quieren olvidar lo convierten en presente de su alma' (III, 112). The cloister, Lorca believes, is appropriate only for those who have lost their vitality; for others it is a torment; the greater the vitality, the greater the torment. As useful context for appreciation of the poem one must reject the notion that convents are necessarily large institutions. In Andalusia they are most commonly small and, from outside, indistinguishable from other houses: whitewashed, with small latticed windows behind which perhaps only half a dozen nuns live in seclusion, devoted to prayer, needlework and, in certain cases, the making of confectionery.

1–4. González Muela has drawn attention to the 'palabras mínimas y precisas' with which Lorca sets the scene: 'La primera palabra nos da la sensación de quietud y paz; la segunda, el color, y un poco de la pobreza del cenobio [...]. La tercera palabra transmite una sensación de color, pero también de olor y frescura.' The observations are clearly justified. But Lorca uses words not only for their immediate resonances of sense and sensation but also for their potentially wider resonances. Silence, for example, suggests 'quietud y paz' but it may also point to restriction and repression.[1] And limewash and myrtle, besides characterising the immediate convent setting, serve also to evoke Andalusia and, more specifically perhaps, Granada (notable for its myrtles; cf. the 'Patio de los arrayanes' in the Alhambra).[2] Moreover, cal, since it is used not only for whitewashing but also for decomposing animal remains, can have death associations (cf. 'dolor de cal y adelfa', I, 161; also 14:30–1) and in the 'language of flowers' so popular in Lorca's day mirto suggests love. Potentially at least, then, the juxtaposition of cal and mirto echoes the duality of vitality and repression already noted in the title. Initially these resonances are merely latent. In retrospect they will seem significant. Amidst the hierbas finas of the convent garden the malvas (another flower of love) appear as a discordant element, perhaps like the nun herself. With easy transition from exterior to interior Lorca presents the girl engaged in a humble task, embroidering gillyflowers on a straw-coloured cloth.

5–8. Evidence that the physical setting is also thematically and emotively relevant here becomes stronger, with birds that seek escape from ensnarement and the church that growls out its bear-like hug. Araña is usually translated or interpreted as chandelier and this is a possible meaning of the word. But a chandelier would be out of harmony with the simplicity and humility of the sort of convent presented and, like González Muela, I prefer to see araña as a cobweb or spider's web, a natural element that also has the advantage of suggesting possible ensnarement, the central theme of the poem.[3] The

[1] La casa de Bernarda Alba, Manchester University Press, 1983, pp xlix–1. The word silencio appears over a hundred times in Lorca's work. A study of its various uses would probably reveal much about his vision and art.

[2] Lorca himself referred elsewhere to both mirto and cal as characteristic Granadine elements: "Me gusta Granada con delirio [...]; vivir cerca de lo que uno ama y siente. Cal, mirto y surtidor' (III, 734).

[3] Compare the following lines in which the poet's heart is seen as a butterfly ensnared by another araña gris:

siete pájaros del prisma are of course the seven colours of the rainbow, refracted in the web (cf. the *siete largos pájaros* in Lorca's 'Canción de las siete doncellas. Teoría del arco iris', I, 273). Visual imagery is succeeded by sound imagery, also in animal form, with bear-like growling from the distant church, presumably the sound of the organ. As befits the restrictive church, the effect of the image is now less pleasant: whereas *vuelan* and coloured birds suggested the enticement of escape (vitality), *gruñe* and *oso* suggest a sombre sound and confining embrace (repression; cf. III, 892–3, for Lorca's dislike of the organ, and I, 478, for an image of the bear's death hug).

9–16. Back to the gypsy nun and her embroidery. *¡Qué bien borda! ¡Con qué gracia!* But the emphasis in the lines that follow is not on what she does embroider but on what she would like to embroider. It is as though, under the impact of sight and sound from outside her cell — flying birds of light and colour that entice and the bear-like church that restricts — she has opted for the birds and given herself up to her own flight of fancy. The flowers that she would like to embroider are more varied and more colourful than the simple ones that she is embroidering and the repeated exclamations serve to emphasise the thrill of her release into fantasy. But for the reader at least they are muted by the repeated reminder of confinement to embroidery: 13 (illusion)-14 (confined), 15 (illusion)-16 (confined).

17–20. The gypsy nun's flight of fancy is here further muted and her sweetening of life's bitterness is reflected in the scent of grapefruits being sweetened in the nearby kitchen (relevant setting again). Appropriately for a nun the bitterness is associated with the sufferings of Christ (the traditional five wounds of the Crucifixion, represented in countless paintings and Holy Week tableaux) and it is this, presumably, that caused the bitter grapefruits to be imagined as five, with further expressionistic moulding of physical reality to her emotive state. An earlier draft of lines 17–18 is revealing: *Olor de limon y azucar / Viene desde la cocina* (*A* I, 144–5). It falls short of the definitive version in two main respects: (1) it juxtaposes bitterness and

> ¡Mi corazón es una mariposa,
> niños buenos del prado!,
> que presa por la araña gris del tiempo
> tiene el polen fatal del desengaño (I, 27).

sweetness but does not show bitterness being sweetened as the gypsy nun herself sweetens bitterness; (2) the *olor de limon* does not parallel and support the *cinco llagas de Cristo*. In both cases, then, the lines are less expressionistic. The change to the definitive version shows Lorca's expressionism to be the result of a sophisticated effort to adapt setting to theme. Apart from the relevance of the bitter/sweet duality to the whole poem (reality/fantasy, confinement/freedom, institutional world/world of nature) two real-life details serve to underpin the imagery: Almeria is noted for its citrus fruits ('Por la calle pasa un hombre vendiendo [. . .]: "naranjas, naranjitas de Almería" ', III, 727) and the making of crystallised fruits is a traditional occupation of nuns in Andalusia. I find myself unconvinced by the interpretation of *llagas de Cristo* as *nasturtiums* (Gili, Cobb).

21–8. The enticement of the world outside continues and the nun appears to see two horsemen ('¿dos, o uno, reflejado en cada ojo, ya que Lorca dice *por los ojos de la monja* y no *por el campo*?', González Muela). As the sound of galloping fades into the distance, a tremor runs through her (akin to the bristling up of an animal; cf. 4:19–20)[4] and she becomes conscious, with breaking heart (a sweet, fragrant heart, very different from the grapefruits which needed sweetening), of her habit as something separate from herself and thus as an element of confinement and repression.

29–32. Back to her yearning. What a steep plain she imagines, bathed in the light of twenty suns! What upraised rivers! One can, if one wishes, associate this on a realistic plane with her sloping embroidery frame, but it is scarcely important. Just as the number of grapefruits in line 17 was prompted by her suffering (together with the traditional association of Christ's wounds) so now the abundance of suns and the steep plain are expressions of her longing (expressionism again). Nature in all its vitality is being evoked from within the confines of her nunnery cell.

33–6. *Pero* (back at last to the reality of lines 3–4) *sigue con sus flores*, whilst the light, on foot (unlike the rivers which she only imagined to be so), plays its chessboard game of lattice shadows (a

---

[4] Cf. Lorca's draft version: *Y siente por sus espaldas / un negro chorro de hormigas (A* I, 144–5).

further pointer to restriction) high up on the wall of her cell. With the last line everything becomes clear. The gypsy nun's only window is too high for her to see the surrounding countryside. She did not actually *see* the horsemen, then. They were projected on her eyes from within, prompted by the sound of galloping (just as the *cinco* in *cinco toronjas* was prompted by the pungent smell and the traditional five wounds), and she longed for a steep plain and upraised rivers so that she could really see them instead of the mere *yertas lejanías* of clouds and mountains. But it is not possible. She continues in her confinement, while the light itself, free from the threatened ensnarement of the *araña gris*, taunts her with a chessboard game of light and shade.

Of the commentaries listed the earliest and latest are the most sensitively text-orientated, but Foster's and Cobb's too are valuable. Correa, usually one of Lorca's most perceptive commentators, is not at his best on this poem and Selig's article is slight. Cano Ballesta, in a two-page comment, overlooks the significance of the key word *quisiera* (11) with its pointer to an abyss between longing and reality and finds 'un bello idilio laboral en el contexto de un mundo utópico'. The gypsy nun, he believes, is a 'prototipo del ser humano *total* en el sentido marxista, en pleno uso de sus facultades creadoras y contraimagen del obrero alienado de la era industrial'; her work is 'un acto humano cualitativo y gratificante, lejos de toda actividad alienada, sólo atenta a lo cuantitativo y calculable de la mercancía'. Bly, wholly eccentric in his emphasis on the interaction of horizontal and vertical planes, finds pointers to a sexual fantasy. His suggestion is that the vertical elements, 'possibly evocative of phallic pleasure', reinforced by the grapefruits, 'symbolizing the enjoyment of the juices of life, sex, the source of life', are relevant to 'sexual arousal' on the part of the nun ('clearly sexual intercourse', 'a flirting with an old boy-friend') and result in manifest 'sexual orgasm' in lines 23–4, probably 'multiple orgasm' in view of the *veinte soles arriba*. More interestingly he notes that José Moreno Villa, to whom the poem was dedicated, was not only a poet and painter but also a champion of Cubism. This may well be relevant to the nun's yearning for a Cubist-type steep plain and for rivers on foot, and it would make the dedication significant, unlike most of Lorca's dedications. It is also relevant to certain of Lorca's own drawings (for example, those for *Mariana Pineda*, akin to Picasso's drawings for Falla's *El sombrero de tres picos*) and to his request, in *Amor de Don Perlimplín* ..., for 'perspectivas [...] equivocadas deliciosamente' (II, 480).

Select bibliography: J. Gónzalez Muela, 'Concentración expresiva en FGL', in *ML* 36 (1954–55), 99–101; Correa, 33–4; K. L. Selig, '"LMG" de GL: ensayo de análisis', in *Cuadernos del Sur* (Bahía Blanca) 11 (1969–71), 226–7; J. Foster, '"LMG": the conflict of two worlds', in *RoN* 17 (1977), 236–40; J. Cano Ballesta, 'Utopía y rebelión contra un mundo alienante: el *RG* de Lorca', in *GLR* 6 (1978), 71–85 (esp. 73–5); P. A. Bly, 'Lines, shapes and distances in "LMG"', in *GLR* 6 (1978), 111–26; Cobb (1983), 73–5; Lisboa, 71–9.

6

LA CASADA INFIEL

A gypsy recounts a sexual adventure with a married woman. It is Lorca's best known and most quoted poem. There are two probable explanations: the eroticism of theme and treatment and the untypically clear narrative progression. In the latter respect a contemporary review by Andrenio (E. Gómez de Baquero), a notable critic of an older generation, is revealing. Lorca, according to Andrenio, was the most gifted poet of the new generation, outstanding for his brilliance of imagination and imagery and for his remarkable musical and visual sense; in short, for the 'elementos y materiales' of artistic composition. But perhaps he should be more selective, more ordered, more disciplined, more respectful of meaning as opposed to mere word music, and more concerned with the elaboration of his poems. 'Que esta elaboración no malogra la flor delicada de la inspiración, sino, al contrario, la hace abrirse con toda su pompa, lo dice, no sólo el buen sentido, sino el mejor de los romances gitanos, que es "La casada infiel", precisamente el más elaborado' (*La Voz*, 6 August 1928). Elaboration, then, for Andrenio, would seem to involve a fuller integration of Lorca's magical 'materiales poéticos' into a clear narrative progression, as in 'La casada infiel', with correspondingly more immediate intelligibility. One suspects that the popular, unsophisticated view of poetry is akin to Andrenio's and that this, together with the eroticism of theme and treatment, explains the special favour accorded to this poem. Lorca himself, supremely concerned with discipline and elaboration, though in a sense very different from that advocated by Andrenio, came to express a different view. But if it is true, as has been stated, that 'La casada infiel' was being recited by Spanish students at the Sorbonne before it was published, we are obliged to assume that Lorca himself frequently recited the poem and that initially at least he was pleased with it. He also selected it (together with the 'Martirio de Santa Olalla') for advance publication in *Revista de Occidente*, the periodical of the publishing house that a few months later was to publish *Romancero gitano.*[1] Later, in public at least, he reacted against the poem, describing it in his lecture-reading as 'gracioso de forma y de imagen' but 'pura anécdota andaluza'. He continued: 'Es popular hasta la desesperación, y como lo considero lo más primario, lo más halagador de sensualidades y lo menos andaluz, no lo leo' (III, 343). It is nevertheless an extremely fine poem and it reveals some of the best qualities of Lorca's writing. Moreover, in private Lorca continued to recite it with enthusiasm.[2] Of all the poems in the book it is the one in which the poet himself is most clearly not the narrator. Two wholly different explanations of the dedication have been given.[3] They are interesting but throw on light on the poem itself.

1–3. The ostensible gypsy narrator, in a mini-prologue that antici-pates the main action, tells of an adventure that he has had with a young woman who turned out to be married. Rizzo quotes four traditional poems of comparable theme (in *Clavileño* 36, November-December 1955, 47) and Francisco García Lorca has recalled that he and his brother heard the opening lines recited by a muleteer during a journey that they made together through the Sierra Nevada, though Lorca himself later had no recollection of this and continued to believe that the opening lines were his own creation.[4] Whatever the facts, for

[1] Further evidence of the poem's rapid popularity: it was written up in manuscript form on 27 January 1926 (*A* I, 146–9) and first published two years later (*RO* 19, no. 55, January 1928, 40–2); but it was already known to Fernando Allué y Morer and his friends when Lorca arrived in Vallado-lid at the beginning of April 1926 for a recital of his poetry (*RO* 32, January–March 1971, 232). Nor was it alone in its impact. As Miguel Pérez Ferrero noted in a contemporary review, even before its publication, *Romancero gitano* had influenced the style of other poets (*La Gaceta Literaria*, 15 August 1928).

[2] Carlos Morla Lynch, *En España con FGL*, 2nd ed., Madrid 1958, p. 438.

[3] C. W. Cobb, 'FGL and the dedication of "La casada infiel"', in *RoN* 8 (1966–67), 165–9; Josephs and Caballero, 245.

[4] Lorca, *Three Tragedies*, Harmondsworth 1961, p. 21. I have myself collected the following *bulería* (relevant to lines 1–2 and 22–3) from Andalusian oral tradition:

> Que yo no me la llevé a la playa,
> que ella se vino conmigo.
> Y por cabecera la puse
> la cola de una caballa [a tunny-like fish].

[contd.]

purposes of commentary we must accept the words as they are, as elements in Lorca's own poem. One is struck immediately by the abrupt opening *Y que*, which suggests that something has gone before. The effect is reinforced by the subtle use of the *romance* form. Basically the *romance* has eight syllables to a line, with a single assonance throughout the even lines. But in this poem the opening line has a syllable too many and the assonance is on the odd lines.[5] It would therefore be more accurate to say that the first seven syllables of the poem are missing. This reinforces the impact of the abrupt opening and serves to project the reader or hearer immediately and with maximum attention into a tale that has apparently already started — as if he were a spectator arriving late at the theatre, says Eich. But he has arrived in time to gather the main point of the gypsy's prologue: that he took a girl down to the river thinking she was unmarried, but she had a husband.

4–15. The drama proper now begins. It was on the night of Saint James (25 July), and almost by obligation. There is a nice duality of meaning: on the one hand the gypsy narrator felt obliged to correspond to the girl's affection (with a reference back to the prologue); on the other hand it almost had to be the night of Spain's patron saint for an adventure such as he is about to relate. Accepting the former meaning and disregarding or rejecting the latter, several critics emphasise the woman as the seducer (at times with reflections on the general human condition) and seek to interpret the poem accordingly. This seems to misinterpret the lines in two respects, both relevant to Lorca's characterisation of his gypsy protagonist as a *fanfarrón* (swaggerer, braggart): in the first place it disregards the mythic stature that he seeks to give to his adventure; in the second place it overlooks his self-enhancing suggestion of sexual irresistibility and favour bestowed. As

The version is imperfect but I quote the words as I heard them, from someone with little or no knowledge of Lorca's poetry. The problem of collecting such material from contemporary oral sources is that one cannot be certain that it predates Lorca and was not influenced by his poetry. Given the evidence of Lorca's brother and the character of my informant, it seems fairly sure that these lines are wholly traditional.

[5] Eich suggests that the first line has *two* syllables too many, for there could be no *sinalefa*, he believes, between *llevé* and *al*. Romero studies the syllabification of the line at length and concludes, as I do, that there are nine syllables. To Romero's evidence can be added that of lines 25 and 50 of the poem where there is *sinalefa* in comparable cases.

we shall see repeatedly in this poem, the gypsy's words have to be taken with a very considerable pinch of salt. The lamps went out and the crickets lit up (6–7), a fine example of hard imagery to indicate transition from the restraining world of civilisation to the unbridled world of nature,[6] and at the furthest corners of the town, another indication of the point of transition, the senses take over: touch (9), with clear evidence that, whatever depth psychology might suggest, the protagonist does not see himself as a 'passive participant' (Maio), sight and scent (10–11), and sound (12–15), with the *diez cuchillos* as a pointer to the gypsy's eager fingers.

16–19. With a change of verb tense that suggests a move forward in time the trees have grown and are no longer seen with moonlight on their branches. It is a good example of how, as in the previous poem, Lorca recreates for us the experience of his protagonists, for the gypsy and the girl are now under the trees, down by the river, and the trees seem correspondingly darker and taller. Lines 18–19 confirm this with a synaesthetic evocation of the distant barking of dogs (far from the river, the present standpoint, emphasised now by the present tense). Notable, too, is the sense of nature's unleashed vitality (trees that have grown and a distant horizon that barks).

20–7. Beyond the brambles, reeds and thorn bushes of the river bank, with a typically Lorcan relaxation of tension at the beginning of what is in fact Act II of this mini-drama (compare any of his tragedies for evidence of a similar relaxation and subsequent build-up of tension), the couple prepare for the sexual act. 'El gitano la desnuda rápidamente junto al río,' writes a distinguished critic (*CHA* 433–4, 1986, 142). But this surely misses the point and overlooks the humorous character portrayal, by a poet who was also a dramatist. So do recorded readings, with their uniformly intense rendering of lines 24–7. Not only does the girl do her own undressing; the contrast between her enthusiastic stripping down (dress, 25, and four petticoats, 27) and the narrator-protagonist's modest removal of tie and revolver, as though

---

[6] Eich assumes that *grillos* give off light and Correa interprets them as *fireflies (luciérnagas)*. But *se encendieron* is surely a synaesthetic rendering of sound. Cf. '¡Cigarra! / Estrella sonora / sobre los campos dormidos' (I, 25); 'Cien grillos quieren dorar / la luz de la cañavera' (I, 325).

for relaxation, suggests eagerness on the one hand and mere com-
pliance on the other. The effect becomes clearer by comparison with
the following traditional lines, with their indication of more equitable
disrobing:

> ellas quitan la su saya
> y yo el mi pantalón;
> ellas quitan su camisa,
> y yo el mi camisón.

Unlike this traditional lover Lorca's gypsy protagonist implies — as
in line 5 — that his own virility is conferred as a favour. Probably,
as C. B. Morris has suggested, he is presenting a cinema-influenced
fantasy image of himself as both lover and cowboy hero, for he would
not really be carrying a revolver and the swaggering *fanfarrón* effect
recalls many a western. But the lover-fighter combination is in any case
frequent in popular literature and Lorca almost certainly knew the
following lines, from the most famous *romance* collection of his day:

> ¡Galiarda, Galiarda!
> ¡Oh quién contigo holgase,
> y otro día de mañana
> con los cien moros pelease! (*RVC* 138),

especially since the immediately following *romance* has lines comparable to the gypsy's ensuing boast and praise:

> Esta noche, caballeros,
> dormí con una doncella,
> que en los días de mi vida
> yo no vi cosa más bella (*RVC* 139).

28–39.   Again we are transported to a world of the senses (akin to
8–15). Touch, scent and sight are invoked to describe the beauty of the
girl's skin (28–31) and her convulsing thighs are likened to startled fish
(32–5; touch and sight), an appropriate image for a gypsy who would
also be a poacher. The climax of the act is presented in terms of yet
another of his occupations — and with another pointer to animal
vitality —, horse-riding (36–9), with *el mejor de los caminos* as a
fanfarrón reminder of his familiarity with this particular type of road.

40–7.   But *Aquella noche* (36) has served also to place distance
between the act and the recounting of it, and this is developed in the

present lines with the gypsy's proclaimed gallant resolve not to reveal the endearing things the girl said to him (40–1). In view of what he has already revealed — and not merely about what she *said* — the resolve is both humorous and character-revealing. His *fanfarronada* consists not only in parading his sexual prowess, but also, afterwards, in presenting himself to his audience as a man of discretion, a claim that is further pressed in lines 42–3. The abstract noun *entendimiento* comes strangely in the context of Lorca's writings, in the same way that the claimed qualities of *entendimiento* and *comedimiento*, however appropriate they might be to the English consul in his white towers, are wholly foreign to Lorca's gypsies, especially to the protagonist of this poem. In that, precisely, lies the humour of the claim. There is scorn now in the gypsy's reference to the girl, filthy with kisses and sand, and line 45, with its distancing switch to the preterite, recalls the opening of the poem and the deception she practised on him. But if she deceived him, his macho self-esteem now encourages him to feel that he merely used her. As they left the place of love, nature, its vitality undiminished, was continuing still, with appropriate sexual imagery, the dual of love that they themselves had abandoned.

48–55. The poem concludes with an eight-line epilogue. The narrator evokes the blood of his race to explain and justify his behaviour, presumably both in the affair itself (already described) and in his subsequent response to the girl's deception (about to be revealed). With swaggering *laísmo* (*La regalé* for *Le regalé*) that goes well with his earlier *yoísmo* (1, 24, 26, 45) he reveals that he paid her for her favours, appropriately with a sewing-basket (a pointer to yet another gypsy occupation, basket-making, and a reminder to the girl of her married state).[7] And lest we should doubt his magnanimity he

---

[7] Luis García-Abrines, 'Sobre un caso de laísmo en GL', in *RHM* 23 (1957), 305–6. The case is convincing but not certain. In a manuscript version of the poem Lorca wrote *Le* (*A* I, 148) but *La* appears in all *RG* editions published in Lorca's lifetime and in the Aguilar *OC* edition. *Laísmo* is not characteristic of Andalusian speech but is extremely characteristic of popular Madrid speech and is especially associated with the swaggering *chulo* of zarzuela tradition. Lorca selects from Andalusian speech only those elements that are both relevant to his total effect and meaningful outside an Andalusian context (the frequent use of the diminutive, for example). The above case of *laísmo* suggests that, here at least, he did the same with Castilian speech. Certainly the bragging effect

emphasises that the basket was large and lined with satin. The poem concludes with a final defence of his ego: the girl did not really deceive him at all, for, in view of the circumstances, he resolved not to fall in love. The affair is over and done with. The final re-echoing of the opening lines presses the point.

I find myself alone in my emphasis on the protagonist's self-revelation as a braggart and on the associated humour, but am otherwise broadly in agreement with Correa (uncharacteristically thin), Eich (the fullest commentary), Nims (short and to the point), Romero (especially the second half), Cobb and Lisboa. Umbral makes three points that either seem obvious or remain doubtful: that eroticism is a clamour for liberty, that it is the woman who seduces the gypsy, and that the protagonist of the poem is not Lorca but a gypsy. Feal Deibe too emphasises woman as the seducer, with much attention to *casi por compromiso* (which he associates exclusively with lines 1–3) and with disregard of lines 8–15 (where the gypsy is clearly the active partner). As for the triumphant ride (36–9) he finds in the mother-of-pearl filly an implicit fear of being devoured by the shell, presumably related to his belief that the sewing-basket (50) is a womb symbol. Maio notes that this poem is different from others in the collection and suggests that the whole sexual encounter was a mere fantasy with 'an imaginary companion created out of the narrator's need to cope with his inability to deal with women'. 'Only in this context is it possible to make room for the gypsy in the *Romancero*'s world of frustration and tragedy'. Maio's attempt to bring the poem into line is understandable and interesting, but hardly supported by Lorca's own dismissive reference to the poem as 'pura anécdota andaluza'.

Select bibliography: Correa, 34–5; C. Eich, *FGL, poeta de la intensidad*, Madrid 1958, 15–36; Nims, 243–6; Umbral, 102–5; H. R. Romero, 'Hacia una reivindicación de "LCI" de FGL', in *ETL* 1 (1972–73), 129–34; Feal Deibe, 63–71; E. A. Maio, 'An imaginary companion in GL's "LCI"', in *GLR* 8 (1980), 102–10; Cobb (1983), 75–6; Lisboa, 81–9.

of *laísmo* is recognised throughout Spain and is here obviously relevant to Lorca's gypsy protagonist (as it was also relevant to the protagonist of the *bulería* that I transcribed in footnote 4 from an Andalusian informant). Lorca's most recent editors (Mario Hernández and García Posada), however, both revert to the manuscript *Le*.

7
ROMANCE DE LA PENA NEGRA

This is one of the finest poems in the book and the one that most closely captures the dark passion and fatalism of Andalusian *cante jondo*. 'En la copla andaluza solloza como en un vasto Miserere todo el dolor irredimible de un pueblo, todo el dolor irredimible de la humanidad, aunque expresado con los acentos de un duelo personal e íntimo.'[1] Lost joy, denied happiness, impossible striving, impending doom, the unending sorrow of human existence — these are the themes of Andalusian 'deep song'. It is elemental, passionate, dramatic ..., but also contained in its pathos and its lamentation. In 1922 Lorca was involved in the organisation of the famous *cante jondo* festival in Granada and both then and later he lectured enthusiastically on the art of *cante*.[2] 'No hay nada, absolutamente nada, igual en toda España, ni en estilización, ni en ambiente, ni en justeza emocional', he declared (III, 205). He emphasised also *cante*'s basic concern with love and death, the 'terrible pregunta que no tiene contestación', the pathos, the absence of half-tone, the night setting, the close identification of woman and *pena* .... The transition to his later comments on 'Romance de la pena negra' is easily made:

> La Pena de Soledad Montoya es la raíz del pueblo andaluz. No es angustia porque con pena se puede sonreír, ni es un dolor que ciega puesto que jamás produce llanto; es un ansia sin objeto, es un amor agudo a nada, con una seguridad de que la muerte (pre-ocupación perenne de Andalucía) está respirando detrás de la puerta (III, 344).

Soledad Montoya's *pena*, then, is the same *pena* that finds expression in *cante jondo*. It epitomises the sorrow of a people but, like *cante*, reveals itself 'con los acentos de un duelo personal e íntimo'. The here-and-now serves, characteristically, as a pointer to the transcendental.

[1] Rafael Cansinos Assens, *La copla andaluza* [1933], Madrid 1976, p. 29.
[2] 'El cante jondo. Primitivo canto andaluz' (III, 195–216), 'Arquitectura del cante jondo' (III, 217–22).

In view of the close relationship of this *romance* to *cante* it is worth noting that the first two lines were originally the opening lines of a poem written in November 1921 for *Poema del cante jondo* but subsequently discarded.[3]

1–4. The mattocks of the roosters are digging in search of the dawn as Soledad Montoya comes down the dark mountain. Comparison with the opening lines of a well-known traditional *romance* illustrates both Lorca's debt to tradition and his strikingly modern exploitation of tradition:

> Media noche era por filo,
> los gallos querían cantar,
> conde Claros con amores
> no podía reposar (*RVC* 190).[4]

Lorca offers similarly brief temporal placing and then, like the anonymous medieval poet, introduces his protagonist. But he departs from tradition in two notable respects: first, in the setting, he brings together darkness and cockcrows in a remarkably modern synaesthetic image in which the crowing (sound) is presented as a digging (sight) in search of the dawn;[5] secondly, this digging in search of the dawn is relevant to Soledad Montoya's own attempted escape from darkness and this will become increasingly apparent as the poem progresses.

[3] *Poema del cante jondo*, ed. Christian de Paepe, Madrid 1986, pp. 7–8, 314.

[4] I disregard the much quoted line from the *Poema de Mio Cid*, 'Apriessa cantan los gallos e quieren crebar albores', for the second hemistich means not 'they [the cocks] want to break the dawn' but 'the dawn is about to break' (cf. above, 'the cocks were about to sing'). Comparison with the quoted *romance* lines, I believe, is more revealing.

[5] Cf. 'Las codornices, antes de nada, dan pequeños aldabonazos en la noche para que abra el alba. ¡Venga golpear la puerta del alba con los nudillos de su canto!' (Ramón Gómez de la Serna, *El alba y otras cosas*, 1923; in *OC* I, 1956, 625–6). Since Lorca's lines were written in November 1921 but not published until after 1923 (in *Proa* of Buenos Aires, date unknown but not before 1924; also in *El Norte de Castilla*, 9 April 1926, and in *Verso y Prosa* 7, July 1927) there is no question here of specific influence. But Ramón Gómez de la Serna (1891–1963) was a notable figure of the Spanish avant-garde and a leading exponent of the sort of imagery indicated. The above juxtaposition thus serves to illustrate the modernity of Lorca's own image.

In other words, Lorca, with a sophisticated modern image, brings together both cocks and darkness to suggest a quest for escape and then shows this quest to be relevant to Soledad Montoya. Both these things involve an intensity of integration that is absent from the traditional *romance*. The night of Soledad Montoya, said Lorca in his lecture-reading of *Romancero gitano*, is a 'concreción de la Pena sin remedio, de la pena negra de la cual no se puede salir más que abriendo con un cuchillo un ojal bien hondo en el costado siniestro' (III, 343–4). The physical darkness of the opening lines, then, is an image of the emotive *pena negra* of the title. The roosters' mattocks, like the knife referred to by Lorca, are instruments of possible release. The name Soledad Montoya is important too. Besides being a typical gypsy name, it serves to associate the protagonist both with the dark mountain (*monte/Montoya*) and with the emotive darkness of her own loneliness (*Soledad*). She too, one feels, is seeking escape from darkness.

5–8. Soledad is now described, with physical characteristics — firmness, colour and small — that suggest also her emotive state — proud (*cobre*) but, since *cobre* is usually 'de color rojo pardo' (DRAE), deprived (*amarillo*), vigorous (*caballo*) but despairing (*sombra*) —, and with an image of her breasts as smoked anvils (strength and despair again, with a suggestion of beating the breast and thence of suffering)[6] which wail round songs (with the superposition of auditory and visual sense perceptions and a transferred epithet, round breasts suggesting round songs). The wailed songs thus appear as a response to everything that has gone before. They are the lament of a woman of vitality in her torment of black sorrow. But Soledad is too proud, too stoical, to utter her own lament. It is her body that tells of her despair, not she (cf. above, comment on 3:5–8: the transfer of fury to the horses).

9–14. Consequently, when the narrator, basing himself on mere appearances (*sin compaña y a estas horas*) and apparently insensitive to the wider resonances, assumes she is simply looking for someone and

---

[6] J. K. Knowlton quotes popular sources for the image of the anvil as an object of beating: 'The image of the anvils in GL's "RPN"', in *RoN* 13 (1971–72), 38–40. On Lorca's use of zeugma in lines 6 and 26 see R. López Landeira, 'La zeugma, figura de dicción en la poesía de FGL', in *RoN* 11 (1969–70), 21–5.

steps into the poem to probe her anguish, he receives a sharp rebuff for his interference, in words that fuse colloquialism and dignity in a way that is difficult to render adequately in English. *Mi persona*, which echoes *cante jondo* and, in harmony with what has gone before, links Soledad's emotive state with her physical being, is especially difficult.[7]

15–18. Lines 13–14 were less abrupt than those preceding and their partial confession encourages the narrator to continue the dialogue. But now he is wary of Soledad's sharp tongue, joins affection with commiseration in line 15 (on the model of popular expressions of endearment such as 'Felipe de mi alma', 'Mari-Pepa de mi vida', 'madre de mi corazón') and warns her only obliquely, as though by proverb, of the danger of unbridled passion (16–18). But the horse image, with its echo of line 6, urges upon the reader the special relevance of the words to Soledad and the verb *encuentra* introduces the possibility of a dangerous resolution to the train of quest emphasised in earlier lines (2, 9, 11, 13).[8]

19–22. Soledad's reply is prompted by the letter rather than the spirit of the narrator's warning. What he was principally warning her of was a metaphorical sea (the feminine *la mar*, with its resonances of 'la mar amarga' and 'la mar de mis desdichas' of traditional Spanish poetry; cf. Lorca himself in 4:24). Soledad, however, interprets the word in its purely physical sense (as the masculine *el mar*) and sets up against it the contrast of the olive lands (with the plural *tierras* to emphasise that they are no mere abstraction) where black sorrow has its true source. As in 'Romance sonámbulo' there is a 'sensación de anécdota' in these lines, a pointer perhaps to love — amidst the fertility of the olive groves — followed by abandonment. It may be relevant, then, that the previous poem was 'La casada infiel' — not of course because Soledad

---

[7] In the narrator's question, as in a dozen other places in *Romancero gitano*, one senses an echo of Cervantes's *La gitanilla*: '— ¿Quién diablos os trajo por aquí, hombre, a tales horas y tan fuera de camino?' (*OC*, 793); 'preguntóle [...] cómo caminaba tan tarde y tan fuera de camino' (*OC*, 794).

[8] One finds similarly pithy admonitions in traditional *romances* — e.g. '¡Harto hace el caballero / que guarda lo encomendado!' (*RVC* 73) — but, as in the compared opening lines, with notably less visualisation and integrating imagery.

was the *casada infiel* but because Lorca now presents seduction and desertion from another viewpoint. This would explain why Soledad, in her obsession at abandonment, has interpreted the narrator's metaphorical sea as a purely physical sea (that carries men away from their womenfolk) and why she views it with such distaste, recalling immediately the source of her grief, beneath the murmur of the olive leaves. But mere anecdote plays little part in Lorca's poetry. The all-important element here is the black sorrow. Its possible cause is merely hinted at, not specified. If it were not this cause, one feels, it would be another, for reality never corresponds to human desires. The *pena negra* is ever close to Lorca's gypsies.

23–34. Soledad's earlier reticence has faded and the poet ventures now to commiserate with her more openly. As in 'La monja gitana' (17–20), bitter fruit serves to press the bitterness of her situation: bitterness of waiting and bitterness of mouth (another zeugmatic juxtaposition of emotive and physical experience, and another suggestion of absent love).[9] Soledad takes up the poet's *¡qué pena!* and develops it with further indications of her anguished waiting for someone's return as she runs from room to room, her braids trailing the floor, looking out from door and window (27–30). Again she utters her lament (31–2), with another transposition of her mental state into terms of physical perception, the blackness of her grief turning her flesh and clothes to jet, and each of these elements, clothes and flesh, then prompts a still further lament at their transformation (33–4). It represents the climax of her confession. The barrier of rebuff behind which she took refuge in lines 11–12 has broken down. Her body still reveals her grief, as it did at the beginning of the poem, but now she herself admits the connection. Soledad's *pena*, I suggested earlier, is the *pena negra* of *cante jondo*. Step by step Soledad herself has become identified with that *pena*, to the point, now, that body and clothes have taken on its blackness. Soledad no longer merely expresses *la pena negra*; now she *is pena negra*. 'La mujer, en el cante jondo, se llama Pena', said Lorca (III, 209). In 'Romance de la pena negra' she is both

---

[9] With the wept tears of lemon in Lorca's poem one can compare the wept tears of blood in the following *cante* lines quoted by Lorca himself: 'Cada vez que miro el sitio / donde te he solido hablar, / comienzan mis pobres ojos / gotas de sangre a llorar' (III, 213).

Pena and Soledad. The echoing of the name *soleá*, one of the most important classes of Andalusian deep song, is surely not fortuitous.

35–8. The dialogue ends with the narrator's prescription for cure, appropriately in terms of gypsy magic, with a suggestion of dawn and morning dew (prompted by the larks). Cleansed body (physical) and tranquil heart (emotional), this is what he urges on Soledad. But the repetition of her name and the use of its full form, recalling line 4, identifies her still with her solitude of *monte oscuro*. Earlier she said, *Vengo a buscar lo que busco, / mi alegría y mi persona* (13–14). Her *persona*, it now appears, is not *alegría*, but *pena*.

39–46. Our attention is turned from the pathos of dark mountain and tormented gypsy woman to the charm and freshness of the dawn, expressed in terms of flounced dress (the leaf-spangled river now visible around the foot of the hill) and a crown of pumpkin flowers (the colour and delight of the morning sky). The dawn that the cocks were digging for in the opening lines has come, albeit with a reminder still, through the colloquial expression *dar calabazas* (lit. 'to give pumpkins'; 'to cold-shoulder [a lover], send packing, reject, spurn'), that for Soledad it has brought no release. Nor does it bring release to the gypsies as a whole. In the final lines the parallel between the search of the roosters and the search of the gypsies as represented by Soledad Montoya is finally broken: the cocks have found their dawn; Soledad Montoya and the gypsies have not. The delight of the dawn urges upon us, by contrast, the persistence (with hidden course and far-off dawn) of the gypsies' own black sorrow.

The commentaries listed are in general along the lines of the above. Only Martin's stands out from this general similarity with emphasis on the poem as an anti-mystic (and basically anti-religious) descent from Mount Carmel. The author cites interesting external evidence but his case rests mainly on the highly improbable interpretation of lines 35–6 as an exhortation to sexual activity.

Select bibliography: Correa, 35–6; L. F. Vivanco, *Introducción a la poesía española contemporánea*, Madrid 1957, 418–24; Nims, 247–50; Zuleta, 261–5; E. Martin, 'La dimension socio-religieuse de *RG*: "RPN"', in *Europe* 616–17 (August-September 1980), 57–70; Cobb (1983), 77–9; Lisboa, 91–9.

8
SAN MIGUEL (GRANADA)

It is usual — and justified — to emphasise the mythical quality of Lorca's poetry. It is also important not to overlook the real-life elements that commonly underpin that mythical quality and explain some of the more difficult images and references. 'San Miguel' is a good example. 'Esto es una romería', commented Lorca when he sent a draft of the poem to Jorge Guillén (9 September 1926; III, 894). In fact it is a very specific *romería*, the *romería de San Miguel*, celebrated annually on 29 September and formerly one of the most important events of the year in Granada, especially in the popular quarter, the Albaicín. From an early hour people converged on the area around the Church of San Miguel el Alto, overlooking the Albaicín, to enjoy themselves and to pay homage to their archangel, captain of the heavenly hosts. The following is from a typical description published in the local newspaper, *El Defensor de Granada*, during the years of the *romería*'s greatest popularity:

> La subida al Cerro y romería del Santo, es una de las diversiones más características de esta capital [...]. Aun antes de que el sol ilumine con sus rayos y alegre con su luz, ya una interminable fila de madrugadores ascienden por las empinadas cuestas que conducen a la ermita en que se venera la imagen del príncipe de las celestiales milicias [...]. La feria se extiende por los alrededores del monasterio, abundando los puestos de turrón y avellanas, alternando con los de frutas, algunas de las cuales hacen su aparición en tan clásico día. Refiérome a los girasoles y castañas (*DG*, 1 October 1898).

Later reports, from about 1910, show enthusiasm mingled increasingly with nostalgia. The *romería*, it is said, is no longer what it was. By the 1920s nostalgia prevails: 'el cerro no estuvo lo animado que en aquellos felices pasados años (para los antiguos), que no volverán' (*DG*, 30 September 1922).[1] Lorca captures this nostalgia in his poem. He also

---

[1] When I visited the church in the 1960s it was a reform school, closed to the general public except on special occasions. A number of *granadinos* to

expresses his view of Granada as turned in upon itself, without 'sed de aventuras', 'falta de acción', 'preciosista', with the Alhambra rather than the palace of Charles V as its 'eje estético'. '[Al granadino],' he says, 'le asustan los elementos'; 'como es hombre de fantasía, no es, naturalmente, hombre de valor'; 'se retira consigo mismo'; 'para oír [su voz] hay necesidad de entrar en los pequeños camarines' (III, 249–52). In contrast to the *agua loca y descubierta / por el monte, monte, monte* (15–16) the water of the Vega of Granada 'no [es] un agua loca que va donde quiere', but 'agua medida, justa', contained in its irrigation channels (III, 320). Saint Michael, we shall see, is similarly confined.

1–4. The poem opens with a typical Lorcan situation: a looking out from confinement to a realm of mystery and fascination, with *barandas* as the springboard, *monte, monte, monte* and *mulos y sombras de mulos* as indications of receding and expanding distance, and *cargados de girasoles* as a pointer to the awaited dawn of illusion (the approaching fiesta, appropriately heralded by sunflowers; with a more varied range of vowel sounds than in the darker, nasalised and resonant lines 1–3). The underlying specific reference is scarcely glimpsed and, except for the light it throws on Lorca's poetic technique, here scarcely matters: stall vendors with their mules are carrying up their wares, epitomised in the traditional *girasoles*, in preparation for the day's festivities.

5–8. The initial emphasis is again on vast uncontoured background (*umbrías, inmensa noche*), with more specific elements thereafter — place (*recodos del aire*), irruptive sound (*cruje*) and pungent taste and smell (*salobre*) — as heralds of the coming dawn. As in lines 1–4 the contrast is aided by contrasting sounds: largely resonant and nasalised in 5–6; more agile and animated in 7–8.

9–16. Reference to the mules' eyes, dimmed with night (5–6), prompts a typical Lorcan leap from immediate reality to cosmos, with an image of cosmic mules whose eyes (the stars) are dimmed not by darkness but by the half-light of approaching day (9–12). And as the white mules of heaven, silently, tenderly, take their leave, the vital

whom I lectured a few years later on Lorca's Granada were unaware of the poet's specific references to the *romería*.

world of nature, here epitomised by water, comes fully alive and, in the light of the new day, runs Pan-like, naked, as though in readiness for some pagan orgy (13–16). As elsewhere in the book there is probably an echo of Cervantes's *La gitanilla*.[2] The final result, however, is characteristic of no one but Lorca.

17–28. So far we have looked out from confinement (*barandas*) to a world of dark mystery promising illusion and seen it evolve, in the light of day, to a world of unfettered vitality. An appropriate realm, one might think, for Saint Michael, captain of the heavenly hosts. But not for Lorca's Saint Michael, and his description of the archangel stands out in notable contrast to everything that has gone before: he is heavy with lace, confined in the alcove of his tower, surrounded by lights as in a religious tableau, a domesticated—emasculated—archangel, delicate and boyish, perfumed and oriental, with echoes of a thousand and one nights. Here, more clearly than elsewhere in *Romancero gitano*, Lorca based himself on specifically observed reality: on Bernardo de Mora's statue in the Church of San Miguel el Alto. Behind the altar a glass screen (*vidrios*) separates the nave from the 'camarín' (*la alcoba de su torre*) where the statue of Saint Michael stands surrounded by four lights (*faroles*). The boyish figure of the saint (*efebo de tres mil noches*), sumptuously attired in female dress, a degenerate form of the Roman military tunic (*lleno de encajes ... enseña sus bellos muslos*), and with a fine plume of feathers on his head (*plumas*), is treading, somewhat delicately, on the prostrate figure of a demonic, tailed Satan, his right arm upraised with three arrows in his hand (*el gesto de las doce*), threatening the demon beneath his feet. But despite this threat to his foe there is no trace of violence in the saint's face: 'no se traduce en el celestial semblante un solo destello de engreimiento ni crueldad, pues sólo se observa en los serenos ojos y en las demás hermosas facciones, la calma, el reposo de los justos, el reflejo del Empíreo' (*DG*, 29 September 1908). Nor is it a very manly face: 'su cara, teniendo el sumun [sic] de belleza, no puede decirse con precisión que lo sea de hombre ni de mujer' (*DG*, 28 September 1926).

---

[2] An old gypsy is speaking: 'Somos astrólogos rústicos, porque como casi siempre dormimos al cielo *descubierto*, a todas horas sabemos las que son del día y las que son de la noche; vemos cómo arrincona y *barre la aurora las estrellas del cielo*, y cómo ella sale con su compañera el alba, alegrando el aire, *enfriando el agua* y humedeciendo la tierra' (*OC* 790; my italics).

Lorca elaborates on this reality and suggests resonances of Granada's Moslem past. Granada's Saint Michael is not the warrior hero of more austere Christian tradition. Esconced in effeminate splendour within his glass-partitioned refuge behind the altar, he is remote from the unleashed vitality of the day that has just dawned. Surrounded by *faroles* (instead of daylight), fragrant with eau de cologne (in contrast to the *agua loca y descubierta* of the surrounding mountains), Saint Michael is distant from nature's flowers, especially perhaps from those *girasoles* that heralded the dawn of his own saint's day and were traditionally brought in tribute to the church.[3]

29–44. The opening line, with its pointer to nature's festive freedom, recalls the earlier indications of daybreak and establishes a similar contrast to the intervening description of Saint Michael. But on a prosaic plane of reality there is no sea; the dancing sea is an image. In the growing light of day the formless mass of the town (*mar*) is given specific limits (*playa*) with a joyful opening of balconies (cf. an earlier version: *Por debajo de la sierra / el mar abre sus balcones*).[4] The shores of the moon (with extension from *mar* to cosmic involvement) lose reeds (a Lorcan pointer to half light and solitude; I, 274) and gain voices. First there are the girls from the popular quarter, hefty-haunched, chewing at their sunflower seeds (a notable come-down from the proffered illusion of line 4);[5] then, enveloped in nostalgia, another form of disillusion that Lorca associated especially with Granada, aristocratic ladies and gentlemen sad for times gone by; finally, with a return to the church, the priest celebrating his two-edged

---

[3] Saint Michael, said Lorca in a wholly different context, 'defiende y evita' (III, 308). With his description of Saint Michael one can compare his drawing of Saint George and the dragon (III, 1073).

[4] I advance the above interpretation with misgivings, for all previous commentators seem to interpret *mar* and *playa* as the real plane and *balcones* as the evoked plane. I prefer to invert the relationship (1) because of the real-life absence of the sea, (2) because my reading appears to fit better into the overall context of the poem (cf. *pierden juncos, ganan voces*) and (3) because Jorge Guillén, well aware of 'Lo inmenso del mar, en vía / De forma por fin humana', was — perhaps significantly — chosen by Lorca as the first recipient of the poem.

[5] Cf. '¡Si vieras cómo está Andalucía! Para andar hay que hacer galerías en la luz de oro como los topos en su medio oscuro. Las sedas brillantes miguel-angelizan los culos de las mujeres opulentas' (III, 920).

mass. But why *el obispo de Manila* and why is his mass two-edged? I
have found no evidence in contemporary accounts (1898 to 1926) that
any bishop or former bishop of Manila (in the Philippines) ever
officiated on Saint Michael's day in San Miguel el Alto. Usually it was
the local priest or the canon of Granada cathedral. But the loss of the
Philippines in 1898 marked the virtual end of Spain's great colonial
adventure, and the juxtaposition *el obispo de Manila / ciego de azafrán
y pobre*, besides epitomising the nostalgia with which the *romería de
San Miguel* was commonly viewed in the 1920s, echoes also, with a
mixture of irony and nostalgia, the passing of Spain's warrior past
(which also had its warrior bishops). More importantly, it also parallels
the contrast between the traditional Saint Michael, 'príncipe de las
milicias celestes', and the effete, orientalised, bedroom-confined *efebo
de tres mil noches*. But there are still more resonances than these.
On this special day the officiating priest would be wearing his finest
vestments, including the golden chasuble, and the ostensible gypsy
narrator, appropriately impressed, might well see him as an exalted
dignatory of the Church and bestow on him a title prompted by two
characteristic associations of the day: the 'Cerca del Obispo' (Bishop's
Enclosure), immediately outside the church, and the 'clásico mantón
de manila' (*DG*, 29 September 1926), traditionally worn by women on
that day. The drawing together of church dignitary and female attire
(not only 'the bishop of Manila' but also 'the bishop in Manila shawl')
would thus set up a further parallel to Saint Michael and his own
effeminate appearance and suggest similar alienation (*ciego* the one;
lejano the other) from the world of vitality *por el monte, monte, monte*.
The priest, like his mass, like Saint Michael, offers two faces: *para
mujeres y hombres*.[6]

45–52. We return finally to Saint Michael, with further emphasis on
his passivity and female attire. In early Renaissance painting he is
commonly depicted with a globe or scales of justice in one hand and a

[6] There is good evidence that Lorca knew the biblical Book of Revelation and he may well have been influenced by it in his transition from
the statue of Saint Michael, with arrows in his upraised right hand, to the
priest pronouncing his two-edged mass: 'And he had in his right hand seven
stars: and out of his mouth went a sharp two-edged sword' (Revelation
1:16). Cf. 'These things saith he which hath the sharp sword with two
edges', *ibid.* 2:11).

sword in the other. In the context of Lorca's poem the *globos* over which he holds sway are appropriately no longer worlds but merely the glass bowls of the *faroles* (with a suggestion also of 'balloons'). As for the odd numbers of which he is king, we know of their magical quality, both for Lorca and in popular mythology, and Saint Michael does hold three arrows in his hand. But there is also an echo of the negative senses of the word *nones*, as in *andar de nones (to have nothing to do)*. Saint Michael is magical and insubstantial. The poem ends with an impression of festive delight — exquisite, ecstatic and oriental — suggestive of Granada itself.[7]

Critical guidance on this poem is somewhat lacking. Terracini, starting from a study of the 'triple reiteración' *por el monte, monte, monte*, makes some good observations. Cobb's commentary is useful but elementary. Lisboa's, as usual, is long, text-based and merits attention. Correa's characteristic emphasis on the interplay of anecdote and myth here suffers from unawareness of the former and possible misinterpretation of the latter. Thus, in lines 3–6 he finds 'una metáfora llena de movimiento animador y de misterio con los "mulos" (sombra) que traen los "girasoles" (luz), los cuales se tornan nuevamente negros al penetrar en la oscuridad' (cf. also his comments on lines 33–4; 'Una metáfora de luz (semillas de girasoles) sella la fusión mítica del elemento humano con el cósmico a la hora de la madrugada'). In all these cases, it seems, Lorca is referring to characteristic elements of the *romería*. But his genius lies very much in his ability to make real-life details the bearers of something wider, and I concur with Correa in finding a remarkable sense of mystery in lines 3–6. Not, however, in his equating of *mulos* with mythical 'sombra' and *girasoles* with mythical 'luz', especially if the sunflowers immediately turn black again. The *girasoles*, typical of Saint Michael's day, are surely to be seen here as images of illusion at the approaching *fiesta*. But illusion fits less easily than light into Correa's cosmic interpretation and he overlooks it. As for the bracketed example (33–4), Correa is simply mistaken. The context itself (especially line 35) makes clear the anti-mythical tone. If the chewed *semillas de girasoles* (the famous *pepitas*) have a wider resonance it is that of vulgarity-inspired disillusion after the promise of line 4 rather than any mythical fusion of man with the cosmos. The

---

[7] 'Primor berberisco de gritos y miradores es la Granada vista desde el Cerro del Aceituno' (III, 331).

whole progression of the poem supports this interpretation. Correa's reading here illustrates the danger of overemphasis on a single critical perspective, even when that perspective is as important and as generally justified as Correa's. Feal Deibe, in his own depth-psychology interpretation, illustrates the danger more clearly. I have indicated in earlier commentaries (1 and 6) the manner of his approach and make no further comment.

Select bibliography: Correa, 36–8; Terracini, 435–8; Feal Deibe, 189–203; Cobb (1983), 79–81; Lisboa, 101–11.

9
SAN RAFAEL (CORDOBA)

This poem is considered to be one of the most difficult in the book: 'perhaps the most difficult of all to interpret' (Cobb), 'quizá el poema más enigmático y difícil de todo el libro' (Josephs and Caballero), 'l'un des plus déroutants du *Romancero gitano*' (Boyer). The identity of the two Cordobas (28, 48) is basic to one's interpretation and has caused special difficulties and disagreements. For Díaz-Plaja, for example, the two Cordobas represent 'la realidad y su imagen', for Bowra 'the noisy town of real life and the celestial town on high', for Henry 'l'aérienne et la réverbérée', for Correa architectural Cordoba and its soul, for Schonberg contrasting individuals, 'une verte personnalité celle-ci [architectural Cordoba] et des adolescents celle-là [Cordoba of reeds]'. Further difficulties are caused by the lack of clear narrative progression, by the imagery and by various cultural references and resonances.

One of the special delights of the poem is the way in which it progresses from *misterio confuso* (14), with appropriate difficulty, to greater clarity as elements are gradually polarised around one or other of the two very different Cordobas, with archangel and fish at the meeting-point. One is reluctant to destroy this effect, but clarity of exposition imposes an initial reference to Cordoba's ages of greatest glory: the first under the Romans (c. 200 B.C. to AD 400) when, as capital of Further Spain (Hispania Ulterior) and later of Baetica (roughly Andalusia), Cordoba became one of the most Romanised cities in the Peninsula, with a notable school of writers and orators whose influence extended to Rome itself; the second under Moslem rule (711 to 1236) when, especially as capital of the Caliphate of Cordoba (929–1031), the city was the centre of Moslem power and culture in the western world, as well as being the greatest intellectual centre in Europe. Cordoba, then, stands out, in Machado's words, as 'romana y mora' and both civilisations have left the imprint of their passing. The duality underlies Lorca's poem and explains many of its difficulties. As a further preliminary it is relevant to know: that the only occasion on which the angel Raphael is named in the Bible is in the Book of Tobit (5–12) where he appears as a guide and counsellor to the young Tobias; that while Tobias was washing his feet in the River Tigris a huge fish leapt from the water and tried to devour him; that at Raphael's bidding the young man caught the fish and killed it and later used its heart and liver to cast out devils from his bride and its gall to cure his father's blindness; that because of this Raphael is revered for his powers of healing and is identified with the unnamed angel of healing who 'went down at a certain season into the pool and troubled the water' (John 5:4); finally, that Saint Raphael is the guardian archangel of Cordoba and that his image abounds in the city, most characteristically as a statue on top of a column (known locally as a *triunfo*).

1–12. The poem opens amidst mystery, with the arrival of closed carriages along the river bank. The imperfect *llegaban* presents action already in progress and thus projects us immediately into that action and suggests *cerrados* as a state without immediate resolution. This increases the effect of mystery and leads easily into the descriptive present tenses that follow. The river bank appears with contrasting features: reeds that suggest softness of line and the smoothed *romano torso desnudo* that points to sculpted form. The *torso* may be an actual Roman statue, but the real-life absence of such a statue, the lack of an individualising definite or indefinite article and the overall context suggest, more probably, that Cordoba itself is here seen as the naked Roman torso. The mystery of the *coches cerrados* remains unresolved, but they are now shown reflected in the water, between sheets of flowers and resonances of clouds. *Maduro* in *cristal maduro* reminds us of the river's long history and *cristal* is commonly used in Baroque poetry to indicate water. Since Lorca's generation virtually rediscovered Spanish Baroque poetry and takes its name, the 1927 Generation, from the tercentenary celebration of the death of Luis de Góngora, Spain's greatest Baroque poet, since Lorca himself, in 1926, lectured on Góngora's imagery, and since, finally, Góngora was a native of Cordoba, it is probable that the word *cristal* (like *ondas*, 3, *nublos*, 8, *nocturno*, 12 ...) was a conscious echo of Cordoba's most revered poet. But Lorca does not merely echo imagery that in a modern context would be worn and ineffectual. What he does is reinvigorate it by recalling also the literal meaning of *cristal*. By its reflection in the water the three-dimensional world of nature appears as an art world of superimposed planes pressed beneath glass (*cristal*): the flowers along the river bank, the carriages themselves and the clouds. But the effect is not only visual and the *resonancias de nublos* echo the earlier resonance of repeated *-on-* sounds in *donde las ondas*. Though we cannot so far affirm it with confidence, it seems that amidst the general mystery of these lines there are signs of a polarisation of elements: on the one hand, the delicate, almost feminine *orillas de juncos* and *láminas de flores*; on the other, the more masculine and resonant *donde las ondas, romano torso desnudo* and *resonancias de nublos*. The children who weave and sing of the disillusion of the world may be weaving in a literal sense but, like Boyer, I am myself inclined to interpret *tejen* metaphorically, in the sense that, as in Lorca's own 'Balada triste' (I, 27–8), they weave their song (with a possible echo of the classical Fates) around the eternal theme of life's disillusion.[1] This bridges a return to the *coches cerrados* of the opening line, with further description that on a plane of mere logic contrasts with the children (young versus old) but in its emotive impact also echoes and develops their song's *desengaño* (*viejos, perdidos*, even *nocturno* which, besides darkness, suggests nostalgic music).

13–26. An adversative *Pero* introduces the city's defiance of the *misterio confuso* so far presented. Though in the darkness the uncontoured architecture of smoke prevails, a marble base makes clear the chaste severity of underlying splendour. One is reminded of the opening duality of soft-lined *orillas de juncos* and hard-edged *romano torso desnudo*. One notes also the firm syntactical structure of the lines, not merely with subordination but also with subordination within subordination (*pues si*). This is unusual in Lorca and therefore especially worthy of note. Apart from reflecting Góngora's own *culto* style, it is as though, by means of syntax, Lorca is setting up a firm structure against the *misterio confuso* of lines 1–12. But firm structure and *casto fulgor enjuto* (with further echoes of Góngora in *casto* and *fulgor*) both contrast with the delicate filigree imagery of the following lines and this in turn contrasts with the obviously Roman *arcos de triunfo* (with an echo also of the *triunfos* to Saint Raphael). The duality suggested in my preamble now seems fairly clear: on the one hand Roman Cordoba, sculpted and architectural, resonant and triumphant (*donde las ondas, romano torso desnudo, resonancias de nublos* [with a

---

[1] Cf. 'Cuando ve llegar a la muerte, el ángel vuela en círculos lentos y teje con lágrimas de hielo y narcisos la elegía que hemos visto temblar en las manos de Keats' (III, 314).

suggestion of pagan gods speaking], *pie de mármol, casto fulgor enjuto, arcos de triunfo*); on the other hand Moslem and Moorish Cordoba, delicate and decorative, mysterious and magical (*orillas de juncos, láminas de flores, la arquitectura del humo, Pétalos de lata débil / recaman los grises puros*). In the last four lines, while the bridge (the famous Puente Romano) blows its Neptune murmurs (echoes of the water under the arches and, perhaps like the *resonancias de nublos*, an echo of Roman paganism — and of Góngora's classical references), tobacco-sellers slip through the broken wall. On a plane of mere anecdote one can perhaps see them as smugglers transporting tobacco from the mysterious *coches cerrados*. But given the Roman/Moorish duality that runs through the preceding 22 lines, the appearance of yet another Roman element (23–4) almost obliges one to find a balancing Moorish element: here, presumably, in the fleeing traders whom Lorca may well have associated with towns across the Straits of Gibraltar. There is another point that seems relevant in view of the syntactical and lexical echoing of Góngora's *culto* style. One of Góngora's best known poems is his sonnet 'A Córdoba', written while he was in Granada. It starts: '¡Oh excelso muro, oh torres coronadas / de honor, de majestad, de gallardía!' and the poet later contrasts this splendour of his native city with the 'ruinas y despojos' of Granada. I find it wholly in keeping with Lorca's much underrated playfulness and high spirits that, as a *granadino* himself, he should here have taken his revenge and shown Góngora's *sublime wall and towers crowned / with honour, majesty and nobility* degenerated into a broken wall used by smugglers for the illicit transport of their wares.

27–38.   Part II of the poem changes from the rare *u-o* assonance (rich in potential for darkness and mystery) to the slightly less rare (and slightly less dark) *u-a* assonance. Many of the elements in Part I will reappear in Part II with clearer polarisation. A single fish in the water joins the two Cordobas, and children whose impassive faces remind us both of their earlier worldly-wise song and of the Cordoban tradition of stoicism undress on the river bank to annoy the fish with ironic question.[2] The juxtaposition of Tobias and fish makes clear the reference to Cordoba's guardian archangel and adds justification and significance to the fish in line 27. As for the much misunderstood ironic

---

[2] It is probably relevant to recall here two other notable writers born in Cordoba: the stoics Seneca and Lucan.

question, the Roman/Moorish duality so far suggested, together with the preliminary contextual information offered on Saint Raphael, imposes its own explanation. The surface of the water is as yet undisturbed, with the fish serenely joining the two Cordobas. But the boys are about to 'trouble the water', like the biblical angel of healing, and they taunt the fish, asking him whether he prefers the imminent broken surface in Roman terms (as a bacchanalian reflection of the flowers along the river bank) or in Moorish terms (as a leaping reflection of the Moslem *media luna* ['Islamismo, mahometismo', DRAE]). One difficulty remains: *Merlines de cintura*. It expresses nicely the magic of lithesome bodies and complements the magic of Tobias. But surprisingly in the context of so many Roman/Moorish dualities Lorca here balances the oriental Tobias with the Celtic wizard of Arthurian legend. I have no adequate explanation. Perhaps one should be content with the magical effect itself.

39–46. Another *Pero* (cf. 13) offers defiance to threatening confusion, with a strikingly Gongorine presentation of the fish (39–40; metaphor, antithesis, chiasmus) and its assurance of column-like equilibrium (41–2; hendiadys).[3] The lines thus bring together biblical fish and *triunfo* column, both of which point to Saint Raphael who is thereafter immediately referred to as *El Arcángel aljamiado*, a clear indication that Lorca sees him as both Romano-Christian and Moorish. Given the unanimous tendency of critics to emphasise the sculptured — and therefore more obvious — Roman elements in the poem at the expense of the more delicate and ethereal — and therefore less apparent — Moorish elements, it is necessary to emphasise the point and to invoke the authority of Lorca's own lecture-reading: 'San Rafael, arcángel peregrino que vive en la Biblia y en el Korán, quizá más amigo de musulmanes que de cristianos, que pesca en el río de

---

[3] It is perhaps relevant to note too that the basic contrast, *dora el agua / y los mármoles enluta* is hendecasyllabic and thus further echoes Góngora (cf. 'Confunde el sol y la distancia niega', *Soledad* I, 196; 'Glauco en las aguas y en las hierbas Pales', *Soledad* II, 958; 'la niega avara y pródiga la dora', *Polifemo*, 80). Dámaso Alonso, the best authority on such 'simetría', finds no influence of Góngora on Lorca's poetry (*Estudios y ensayos gongorinos*, Madrid 1955, p. 573). The present poem, appropriately on Góngora's own native city, shows that here at least there was influence. Even the *misterio confuso* from which Lorca starts recalls the *soledad confusa* of Góngora's own starting-point in the *Soledades* (Dedicatoria, 3).

Córdoba' (III, 344).[4] Saint Raphael's *lentejuelas oscuras* are more
sombre than Saint Michael's *espejitos y entredoses* in the previous
poem, but the two dresses are basically alike and they point to the
same oriental heritage. Having been presented as the incarnation of
the Roman/Moorish duality that has gradually evolved out of the
poem's earlier *misterio confuso*, Cordoba's guardian archangel can
now withdraw, approriately to seek repose at the conciliatory meeting-
point of the waves, lulled by their murmur.[5] The imperfect tense
buscaba to mark his withdrawal balances the imperfect *llegaban* with
which the poem opened and serves to give distance to the action and
completeness to the poem.

47–50. The final quatrain is a form of epilogue. It superbly balances
lines 27–30, and lines 29–30 and 49–50 are especially notable for their
Góngora-like symmetry. In each case the first line refers to Moslem
Cordoba and the second to Roman Cordoba. But as though influenced
by the guardian archangel *en el mitin de las ondas* they are now brought
more closely together. Syntactically line 29 (Moslem Cordoba) corresponds to line 50 (Roman Cordoba) — adjective + Cordoba + adjec-
tive/adjectival phrase — and line 30 (Roman Cordoba) to line 49
(Moslem Cordoba) — Cordoba + adjectival phrase. The surface

[4] Without reference to Lorca an authority on Cordoba has made a
similar point: 'En la figura de San Rafael, interpretada a la cordobesa,
[...] se juntaron la tradición local católica y lo musulmán, ya que el
Arcángel resultaba igualmente sacro para los creyentes de las dos clases'
(Rodolfo Gil Benumeya, 'Las luces y las piedras de Córdoba', in *Clavileño*
21, May–June 1953, 70).

[5] The strangeness of the word *mitin* has been pointed out but not
explained. Góngora, we know, was noted for his use of Latinisms. 'Hoy,'
wrote Gerardo Diego in his famous *Antología poética en honor de Góngora*
(1927), '[Góngora] habría tomado su nuevo léxico poético del inglés o el
francés'. Lorca's use of the Anglicism *mitin* is perhaps another conscious
Gongorism to be added to the dozen already noted in this poem. Moreover, in retrospect the list of Lorca's apparent Gongorisms can be leng-
thened, for I have referred above to only the most striking examples. Thus,
in the opening lines alone, alongside *ondas*, *cristal* and *resonancias de
nublos*, one might add anaphora in *Coches cerrados .... / Coches que ...*,
resonant assonance in *donde las ondas*, echoes of both art and classical
antiquity in *romano torso desnudo*, the stylisation of nature in 6–8 (with
another art form and the first of several *esdrújulo* — proparoxytonic —
words in *láminas*) ....

meaning of lines 47–50 is immediately apparent and presumably accounts for the common tendency to see the whole poem in terms of real city versus reflected city. But this duality leaves unexplained many elements in the more difficult earlier part of the poem and suggests only a visual contrast without special relevance either to Cordoba or to Saint Raphael. What I have here principally attempted is to show that *Córdoba quebrada en chorros* is in fact an image of Moslem Cordoba and *Celeste Córdoba enjuta* an image of Roman Cordoba, that almost everything in the poem can be explained as an aspect of this broader duality, that the duality is meaningfully balanced by Lorca around the city's guardian archangel, and that thereby the whole poem gains in significance. What has hitherto been seen in mainly visual terms — except by neo-Freudians in search of homosexuality — in fact epitomises the dual spirit of Cordoba and, beyond that, of Andalusia. Nor is the duality relevant only to this poem. Lorca himself made the point:

> Desde los primeros versos [of *RG*] se nota que el mito está mezclado con el elemento que pudiéramos llamar realista, aunque no lo es, puesto que al contacto con el plano mágico se torna aun más misterioso e indescifrable, como el alma misma de Andalucía, lucha y drama del veneno de Oriente del andaluz con la geometría y el equilibrio que impone lo romano, lo bético (III, 342).

Finally, the duality is perhaps relevant also to conflicting human drives that much concerned Lorca, both as a man and as an artist: passion and control, yearning and containment, inspiration and form, 'gracia de Dios — o del demonio —' and 'técnica y esfuerzo' (III, 402).

Among the commentaries listed Boyer's is the most sensitive, comprehensive and text-orientated, with glimpses also of the influence of Góngora. Hall surveys various interpretations, is healthily condemnatory of two Freudian commentaries and offers useful background information on Tobias and Saint Raphael. His suggestion that the *niños* (9) are seminarists and that the theme of the poem is repressed sexuality is less convincing. Bates offers little more than paraphrase. For Cobb 'the usual criticism has not even approached Lorca's purpose [in this poem]' (1967) and he seeks to fill the gap with unusual criticism. The closed coaches, 'generally a womb symbol', probably mean in this poem that 'the feminine is absent in the struggle which follows'; the ten murmurings of Neptune suggest that the bridge is homosexual; 'at the private level the reeds-architecture symbols had special meaning, the reeds (as phallic) suggesting vitality and Lorca; the architecture, artistic creation and Dalí'; the boys in Part II are 'at that moment of Oedipal struggle when they are suspended between manhood and regression'; with Raphael's help Tobias was successful in that struggle, but Raphael has here become Moorish and is 'unable to help the lads achieve normal manhood'. Other related symbolic suggestions in the poem are passed over as 'too obscure and personal for convincing interpretation'. The basic and recurrent suggestion is that the poem offers Freudian pointers to homosexuality, a view that persists in Cobb's 1983 commentary with the added suggestion that 'the lads and their struggle against the traditional civilized class of the closed coaches represents the central theme of the ballad'. Lisboa's commentary, as always, is reliably perceptive, with brief pointers also to the Rome/Islam duality.

Select bibliography: M. Bates, 'GL's "SR(C)"', in *The Explicator* (University of South Carolina) 24 (1965–66), no. 42; Cobb (1967), 71–2; J. B. Hall, 'Lorca's *RG* and the traditional "romances viejos" with especial reference to "SR(C)"', in *Studies of the Spanish and Portuguese Ballad*, ed. N. D. Shergold, London 1972, pp. 141–64 (esp. 155–64); D. Boyer, 'A propos du "Romance de SR" de FGL', in *LNL* 70, 4 (1976), 60–75; Cobb (1983), 81–3; Lisboa, 113–22.

10
SAN GABRIEL (SEVILLA)

Saint Michael, though not the patron saint of Granada, is — and especially was — much venerated in the popular Albaicín quarter of the city. Saint Raphael, though not the patron saint of Cordoba, is the city's guardian archangel and its most popular saint. To complete his triptych Lorca needed a poem to the third of the archangels, Saint Gabriel, and, presumably also, to Seville. But Saint Gabriel is not specially associated with Seville and suggestions that it is his statue that looks out from the pinnacle of the Giralda tower are mistaken. As the angel of the Annunciation (Luke 1:26–38) Saint Gabriel could most readily be presented in an Annunciation scene, and the patron saint of the archdiocese of Seville, Nuestra Señora de los Reyes, serves as the necessary link, being presented at the moment of Saint Gabriel's appearance to her. But there is none of the cultural perspective that one commonly associates with Western art of the eighteenth and nineteenth centuries. Lorca does not attempt to create a historically accurate scene. As in early painting — and as in the art of less historically conscious communities today — what matters is the contemporary relevance and immediacy of the scene. As Fra Angelico in the fifteenth century depicted his Annunciations in a wholly fifteenth-century context (dress, hairstyle, book of hours, Brunelleschi-type loggia) so Lorca, as an ostensible gypsy narrator, presents his Annunciation in local and contemporary gypsy terms: Saint Gabriel is a delightfully dandified Sevillian gypsy boy and the Virgen de los Reyes has become a local gypsy girl, Anunciación de los Reyes. As befits the theme, it is the most joyous poem in the book. It is also the most jauntily seductive. I reject entirely suggestions that the poem is blasphemous (Cobb), demonic (Umbral) or burlesque (Harris). It has the sophisticated naiveté and charm of an early Renaissance painting.

1–10. In Lorca's *romances* four-line periods predominate, and the opening of the next poem will demonstrate how a four-line period may serve progressively to enhance a protagonist, with climax and release as the verb finally appears in the fourth line. Here the presentation is similar but with a six-line build-up. One notes especially the non-realistic, stylising imagery which serves both to detach the so far unidentified *bello niño de junco* from prosaic reality and to emphasise his idealised gypsy beauty, and the culminating sixth line which resolves the period and, with *ronda* (*roams, walks about*) and the singular *calle*, echoes the best known of all *sevillanas* (a Seville form of *cante*), 'Ronda mi calle. / Ole, ole. / Ronda mi calle'. This releases the secondary meaning of *rondar* (*to roam the streets and pay court to the girls at their window grilles*), a meaning obviously relevant to Lorca's handsome gypsy youth, and serves tacitly to epitomise him as an archetypal *sevillano*. The dandified description continues, with patent leather shoes that crush the dahlias of the air and, with their smallness, colour and sound, appear as brief celestial dirges.

11–22. On the whole seashore (with a sense of vastness and uplift in the departure from the more ordinary *A orillas del mar*) there is no palm tree his equal (with a suggestion of stately elegance — 'This thy stature is like to a palm tree', Solomon 7:7 — and an echo of palms of glory and triumph) nor crowned emperor nor wandering star (both frequent in Andalusian speech and song as pointers to status and illusion).[1] Having elevated his protagonist by measurement against — and proclaimed superiority to — successive elements of distinction, Lorca proceeds to elevate him further by evidence of homage from the world around: first, personified night (17–18); then, guitars stirred to life as if by magic (19). It is at this point that the full name and title first appear: *San Gabriel Arcángel* (20). *Domador* in the following line is normally associated with unbroken horses or wild animals, but the annunciating archangel is here a tamer of little doves, suggesting gentleness but also recalling innumerable early paintings of the Annunciation where doves represent the descent of the Holy Spirit.

[1] One thinks, for example, of José Zorrilla, in 1889, being solemnly proclaimed 'Emperador de la Poesía' in Granada, and of Antonio Chacón, in the festival of 1922, being proclaimed '"emperaor" del cante jondo', and of Lorca's own father telling his son that if only he would pass the odd university examination 'yo te dejaría marchar a Madrid con más alegría que si me hubieses hecho emperador' (III, 700). As for *lucero*, we shall find further evidence, but the following lines from a children's rhyme are relevant: 'lucero del alma mía, / lucero de mi querer'.

Since willows are associated with lamentation and Saint Gabriel brings glad tidings, he is naturally *enemigo de los sauces* (22).

23–6. The narrator intervenes to remind the archangel of his mission (in words that hardly support Correa's notion that annunciation and conception coincide, Saint Gabriel being the father). He will surely wish to reward the gypsies who clothe his image in church by choosing a gypsy Virgin.

27–38. After the elevated, stylised presentation of Saint Gabriel, lines 23–6 have served to bring us back close to real-life normality and Part II opens with the appearance of Anunciación. *Mal vestida, abre la puerta* and *por la calle* keep us close to reality. But there is elevation too, initially in the name itself: *Anunciación* associates the girl immediately with her unique destiny, *Reyes* is a typical gypsy surname that serves to emphasise her lineage, and the whole resonant and regal-sounding name suggests distinction and nobility. Anunciación is no ordinary gypsy girl, it seems. The implication already is that she is blessed among gypsy women. But there is more to the name than this. Seville's patron saint, we have seen, is Nuestra Señora de los Reyes. Anunciación's name, then, serves not only to associate her with her destiny of highly favoured motherhood and to emphasise her gypsy lineage; it also identifies her with Seville's patron saint and associates her with the Virgin Mary at the moment of her own Annunciation. Moreover, like Saint Gabriel, Anunciación is further exalted by the echoing of Andalusian *cante*, this time one of the best known of traditional *peteneras*:

> ¿Dónde vas, linda gitana,
> tan compuesta y tan bonita?
> Voy en busca de un lucero
> que el sentío a mí me quita.

The similarity to the presentation of Anunciación in lines 27–30 is striking and surely not fortuitous. One notices, first, the same assonance in *í-a* (to which Lorca has just changed after the presentation of Saint Gabriel with *a-e* assonance), secondly, the similarly structured second line (adverb-adjective *y* adverb-adjective), thirdly, the word *lucero* which occupies the same final position in both third lines and serves as a similar image of illusion. The consequence of these various *petenera* resonances in Lorca's lines is to bring the remaining elements closer together. In the first line the parallel of *Anunciación de los Reyes* and *linda gitana* serves to reinforce Anunciación's gypsiness and to make of her, more clearly still, the archetypal *linda gitana*, and in the last two lines the intoxication of *el sentío a mí me quita* is carried over to suggest Anunciación's own bewildered response to her herald of good tidings. Lorca's lines, then, both echo the *petenera* and gain strength from it. The gained strength involves an increased impression of stature, of typical gypsiness, of significance and of universality. Immediacy is still important, but now it has transcendental overtones. As in lines 29–30 (*abre la puerta al lucero / que por la calle venía*) domestic realism can henceforth mingle appropriately with cosmic symbol. Saint Gabriel, between lily (the traditional flower of the Annunciation depicted in countless paintings) and smile (cf. *enemigo de los sauces*), great grandson of the Giralda (proud Sevillian heritage), *se acercaba de visita* (with a nice mingling of stately progression, *se acercaba*, and casual colloquialism, *de visita*). As in lines 1–6 the subject finds its verb — and the tension is resolved — only in the final line (34). Hidden crickets suggest the excited fluttering of a heart and the stars turn to *campanillas: bellflowers*, in harmony with the stylised flower imagery that runs through the poem, but also *little bells* appropriate to the forthcoming good tidings and a reminder, perhaps, to the aware reader of the *campanilleros* of Seville who call out the faithful to pay homage to the Mother of Christ on the mornings of her Rosary.[2]

39–62. The dialogue between Anunciación and Saint Gabriel has all the elegant simplicity and sophisticated naiveté of a Fra Angelico Annunciation. One notices, for example, the alternating four-line coplas of the dialogue, the carefully balanced first line of each of Anunciación's utterances (39, 47, 55), the repeated first line of each of Saint Gabriel's announcements (43, 51, 59), the incantatory repetition of the earlier *bien lunada y mal vestida* (52), the flower imagery (41, 50), the exquisite and peculiarly Andalusian colloquialism of *aquí me tienes* (39), *Morena de maravilla* (44), *un niño más bello / que los tallos*

---

[2]   A tu puerta están las campanillas
      ni te piden ellas ni te pido yo
      que te pide la Virgen María
      con el Patriarca y el Niño de Dios.

('Los campanilleros', in *Sevilla y la Semana Santa, Año 1925*, Seville 1925, n.p.)

de la brisa (45–6), *¡Ay San Gabriel de mis ojos!* (47) and of the
repeated — and characteristically diminutive — expression of endearment, *¡Gabrielillo de mi vida!* (48, 56). But the *tres clavos de alegría*
(40) and their echo in the foretold *lunar y tres heridas* (54) call for
special comment. In the former case joy prevails, though the *clavos*
remind us also of the traditional three nails of the Crucifixion (depicted
in numerous paintings); in the latter case the ominous effect of the
foretold wounds prevails, though a *lunar* (echoing *bien lunada* in lines
28 and 52) is considered a good omen in gypsy folklore.[3] There is ambiguity, then, but with evidence of an overall darkening of portents.[4]
I find similar ambiguity in Saint Gabriel's leave-talking: Anunciación
will be mother to a hundred dynasties, both in a religious sense and
with a pointer to gypsy clans, and her eyes reflect landscapes that
suggest both Andalusia and the harshness of her destiny.

63–70. The forthcoming birth has been announced and the child
sings in his mother's womb, with a now clearer suggestion of suffering
in *Tres balas de almendra verde* (bullets of bitterness). Saint Gabriel
climbs a ladder to heaven, with a neo-primitive echo of the ladder in
Jacob's dream: 'set up on the earth, and the top of it reached to
heaven: and behold the angels of God ascending and descending on

---

[3] I take advantage of the point to indicate two further possible echoes of
Cervantes's *La gitanilla* — from a poem in which Preciosa reads a lady's
fortune:

> tendrás un hijo canónigo;   Un lunar tienes, ¡qué lindo!
> la iglesia no se señala (780)   ¡Ay Jesús, qué luna clara! (780)

[4] At the moment of the Annunciation Lorca recalls also the agony of
the Crucifixion. In my commentary on Poem 13 I shall point to further
evidence of such temporal superposition, with a similar bringing together
of the joy of Christ's birth and the suffering of his death. For the moment
I simply draw attention to Carlos Bousoño's study of the device with
reference to his own poem 'Cristo adolescente' (*Teoría de la expresión
poética*, 6th ed., Madrid 1978, I, 394–5) and point to an identical
superposition of present joy and foretold suffering in Lorca's response to
Dalí: 'Me conmueve; me produce Dalí la misma emoción pura (y que Dios
Nuestro Señor me perdone) que me produce el niño Jesús abandonado en
el Pórtico de Belén, con todo el germen de la crucifixión ya latente bajo las
pajas de la cuna' (1927; III, 968). As was suggested earlier, 'under life's
happier appearances lies constantly, for Lorca, its inevitable tragedy'
(Poem 4, p. 29).

it' (Genesis 28:12).[5] In harmony with the poem's stylising flower imagery, the stars that earlier changed to *bellflowers* (and *little bells*) appropriate to the archangel's glad tidings now turn to everlasting flowers, eternalised in their beauty by the Annunciation. But in an Andalusian context — and in the context of Lorca's poetry — it is difficult to escape also the death association of the *siempreviva* ('Siempreviva de la muerte, / flor de las manos cruzadas', II, 936). As with the repeated three wounds, even amidst joy tragedy threatens.

Relatively little has been written on this poem. Umbral offers almost no textual commentary but, in a general survey of the three archangel poems, develops an important aspect of his view of Lorca as a 'poeta maldito' and for this reason alone merits consideration. Lorca's 'manera esteticista, humanizante, desacralizada' of dealing with themes that are 'en cierto modo' religious, he says, proves that Lorca's own religious experience was 'mera sugestión plástica, literaria, anecdótica, verbal y nada más'. Lorca, he believes, lacked faith and his attitude to sacred matters is 'puro demonismo'. For reasons such as these Lorca is to be seen as a 'poeta maldito'. But Lorca's 'mezcla de paganización, esoterización y regionalización de lo religioso,' he continues, is characteristic also of Andalusia, 'tierra daimónica', where Christianity is transformed into 'superstición y conjuro'. Paradoxically, Umbral believes, such 'paganización, esoterización y regionalización' are the three pillars of Christianity, for without them Christianity becomes a universal abstraction and leads to atheism. Christianity, it seems, according to Umbral, cannot win: either it is localised (and therefore pagan) or it is universalised (and leads to atheism). He may well be right, but with this method of argument it is difficult to see how Lorca could ever convince him that he held sincere religious beliefs. The fact is, of course, that he did not try. To read his three archangel poems as though they were a lyrical self-confession, with the author

---

[5] Jacob's ladder is widely represented in Christian art and in the Middle Ages 'was regarded as a "type" of the Virgin Mary, through whom a union of heaven and earth was accomplished' (J. Hall, *Dictionary of Subjects and Symbols in Art*, London 1974, p. 164). It was thus associated with the Annunciation and the Nativity. Lorca, much influenced by fifteenth-century painting, echoes the image again in his evocation of the death of Góngora: 'Poco después, su alma, dibujada y bellísima como un arcángel de Mantegna, calzadas sandalias de oro, al aire su túnica amaranto, sale a la calle en busca de la escala vertical que subirá serenamente' (III, 247).

wholly identified with the ostensible gypsy narrator, is surely mistaken and overlooks the importance of dramatic detachment. It also overlooks the poet's deliberate neo-primitivism. In these poems as elsewhere in the book Lorca projects himself into the gypsy's world of illusion and disillusion, mystery and superstition, and recreates it, intensified, for the sophisticated reader of the present and future. But there is no evidence that he himself fuses with that world. 'Confunden mi vida y mi carácter. No quiero de ninguna manera. Los gitanos son un tema. Y nada más' (III, 902). In contrast to Umbral's treatment Durán Medina's, in the published version of her doctoral thesis, is discreet and text-orientated, with invoked support from Flys, Ramos-Gil, Zardoya and Lara Pozuelo. Cobb finds sexual significance in Lorca's imagery and thence 'a blasphemous attack against the Christian dogma of the Virgin Birth'. Lisboa, close to the text as always, offers the most comprehensive and perceptive of the commentaries listed.

Select bibliography: Umbral, 107–13; Durán Medina, 127–36; Cobb (1983), 83–5; Lisboa, 124–34.

11

PRENDIMIENTO DE ANTOÑITO EL CAMBORIO EN EL CAMINO DE SEVILLA

According to Lorca's friend Morla Lynch this and the following poem were based on a real-life gypsy horse-dealer, a notable horseman and drunkard, who was found dead one morning, apparently pierced by his own knife as he fell from his horse in a drunken stupor (*En España con FGL*, 23–4). The evidence is slim, but consideration of the possibility helps one to appreciate, by contrast with the sordidness of real-life incident, the distinctive and highly distinguished qualities of Lorca's poems. In view of the notable dramatic progression of the 'Prendimiento' the dedication to Margarita Xirgu may well be significant.

1–8. The opening lines are superb: resonant gypsy names, a proud declaration of lineage that echoes epic and ballad literature, a *vara* (*rod, staff, switch*) that amidst so much elevation of tone suggests a staff of office or authority ('vara de alcalde', 'vara de juez') but proves to be a pliant willow switch (with the consequent suggestion of easy acceptance of nobility by a correspondingly pliant, easy-going character), and an extremely effective fourth line that associates Lorca's gypsy of gypsies with *the* city of fiestas and *the* fiesta of fiestas.[1] Every element, then, besides serving to present an individual character, sets up wider resonances. The tone, appropriately, is noble, elegant,

[1] I study this at greater length in a commentary listed below and in the Introduction to my edition of the text. The first two lines, for example, by emphasising gypsy names and lineage, elevate Antoñito to the status of archetypal gypsy. By echoing the presentation of heroes in traditional *romances* (especially *romances moriscos*) they elevate him also to the status of archetypal hero. In the opening lines of the 'Prendimiento' I find at least five similarities to *romances moriscos*: resonant names, proud lineage, festive activities, *cante*-like build-up and release of tension, and the use of four-line periods (in contrast to the more purely narrative Castilian *romance* where two-line periods predominate). Four of these five similarities are illustrated in each of the following two passages (with number references to *Romancero general*, ed. Angel González Palencia, Madrid 1947):

proud, almost arrogant. The fourth line especially one can scarcely read without a swagger. Lines 5–8 describe Antoñito more closely: his olive complexion (with a suggestion also of dreams and fate in the *verde luna*), his proud, easy gait, his glossy locks hanging over his forehead (with a hint of peacock ostentation — 'pavón', 'pavonada' — in the colour of the hair) — a model of gypsy beauty, grace and elegance.

9–16. Description and progressive action are interrupted: first by concentration on a specific point in Antoñito's journey (an extremely significant point that again echoes ballad literature); then by concentration on a specific moment in time (by the shift to the preterite *cortó*). In such a context the action itself stands out as significant and is made still more so by the parallel *a la mitad del camino* (13) which heralds a balancing of action (10–12) with retribution (15–16). As for the action itself, it reveals admirably Lorca's ability to present character without abstraction (in this case, Antoñito's carefree delight in magic — and his lack of more austere practical considerations — as he turns the water in the irrigation channels to gold). The civil guards, in contrast, are presented not as individuals but as a collective force, uncontained even by a definite article (15), and with a corresponding singular verb (16). At this moment, then, and in this place (with a

> Celín, señor de Escariche,   Zulema, al fin, el valiente,
> y Aliatar, Rey de Granada,   hijo del fuerte Zulema [...],
> Azarques y Abenhumeyas   fue a ver en Avila un día
> salen a juego de cañas.   las fiestas como de fiesta.
>   (*RGen* 630)   (*RGen* 700)

To the above similarities can be added, also in the opening lines, Antoñito's character-revealing *vara de mimbre* which likewise echoes *romances moriscos*: '[El Tarfe] sólo lleva por empresa / un verde ramo apazible' (*RGen* 137); 'La gruesa lança de fresno / parece en sus manos mimbre' (*RGen* 657). Other types of *romance*, I find, though clearly relevant, offer fewer direct similarities.

Jeremy C. Forster ('Posibles puntos de partida para dos poemas de Lorca', in *RoN* 11, 1969–70, 498–500) suggests the following *vito*, probably itself a distant echo of the *romance morisco* tradition, as a more immediate source for Lorca's opening lines:

> Una malagueña fue
> a Sevilla a ver los toros
> y a la mitá del camino
> la cautivaron los moros.

further echo in line 14 of countless *romances*) Antoñito, carefree and
magical, is escorted away by the forces of law and order.

17–28. The first sixteen lines are akin to the first act of a play. In Act
II nature takes over from Antoñito as the main protagonist. It also
takes over several of the elements so far used to characterise the hero:
the easy-going *anda despacio* (6) is balanced by the day's *se va despacio*
(17), the fiesta that he was hoping to see now appears as cape-play
of the day with lengthening shadows, and the water that he turned to
gold is recalled in the evening light on sea and streams. Amidst the
expectancy created by the olives' waiting for the magically significant
night of Capricorn (a reminder of Lorca's self-confessed inclination to
associate 'hechos vulgares' with 'imágenes astronómicas', III, 342), a
short equestrian breeze leaps over leaden hills. Nature, then, having
associated itself with the earlier description of Antoñito, now points
to the expected response and shows, by means of the breeze (with
possible grim wordplay on *corta*), how easy it would be for this gypsy of
gypsies to make his escape (over leaden hills, which suggest the civil
guards, *de plomo las calaveras*, 15:6). But the expectation is frustrated
by Antoñito's meek submission to arrest, and parallelism and contrast
serve to emphasise the sense of letdown: first, the repetition of lines
1–2 to remind us of the hero's proud lineage (25–6); then a series of
contrasts to lines 3–4 to bring out the betrayal of that lineage: *sin vara
de mimbre* (deprived) in contrast to *con vara de mimbre* (affirmative);
viene ... entre (confined) in contrast to *va ... a ver* (outward-looking);
tricornios (abject) in contrast to *Sevilla* and *toros* (noble). The word
tricornios is especially effective: apart from the essentialising and
debasing metonymy, made even more debasing by the repeated *i-o*
sounds, the exaggeratedly rich rhyme with *Capricornio* (perhaps the
most powerful justification, in retrospect, for the use of this word)
serves humorously to bring out the contrasting registers of the two
words (on the one hand, a fate-guiding 'imagen astronómica'; on
the other, the debased, real-life arbiters of human destiny) and emphasises the *cuerno* element that is present in both of them (further
debasement of the civil guards as well as an echo of the bullfight,
especially since the corresponding position in lines 1–4 is occupied by
the contrasted *toros*). There is a final reminder of Antoñito's heroic
stature (and an echo of a traditional *romance*) in the fact that he has
five guards, but the overall impression of him as a prisoner of the
tricornios is one of disgrace.

29–38. As though unable to contain himself longer before the gypsy
hero's submission, the narrator, like a Chorus in Greek tragedy ('Who
will, who could absolve you?', Aeschylus, *Agamemnon*, 1509), re-
bukes his protagonist: 'If you were a Camborio you would have killed
your captors. But you have not done so; therefore you are not a Camborio.' The argument is simple but fundamental for an understanding
of Lorca's elemental world of heredity-in-blood in which sons share
the characters and fates of their fathers and daughters the characters
and fates of their mothers. In such a context Lorca's variation on a
common insult in line 33 takes on special significance and *legítimo* in
line 34 brings together both technical and colloquial senses of the
word. But this is no gutter Spanish and, though the speaker is ostensibly a gypsy, there is no gypsy *caló* and no attempt to reflect popular
Andalusian pronunciation. The tone, as ever in Lorca, is elevated
and distinguished. In the poet's own words, 'es un arte, no diré aristocrático, pero sí depurado' (III, 558). The Chorus ends with hard
imagery to evoke the passing of valour and the anger of the dead
gypsies of old (with metonymy that associates them with knives rather
than with mere willow switches).

39–46. The structure of Act III balances that of the action part of Act
I (9–16), after the opening presentation of protagonist, circumstances
and personality. As in lines 9–16 so also here there are two four-line
units, each beginning with the same indication of a significant moment.
As in Act I also there is both balance and tension between the two
coplas: balance between the first lines, which emphasise the same
moment (39, 43) and carry the basic narrative (40, 44), and tension
between the later lines, which open vistas on contrasting attendant
circumstances. In lines 41–2 the civil guards, in an elemental world
where wine and brandy are commonly associated with vitality, drink
lemonade.[2] We are reminded of the lemons that Antoñito was throwing into the water in the corresponding lines of Act I. For the ostensibly
gypsy narrator, the 'civiles' are thoroughly practical and Antoñito's
delight in visual alchemy is foreign to them. The half-playful, half-
scornful suggestion is that they salvaged the lemons and are now
enjoying their spoils. In the last two lines of the poem our attention is
directed once more to the surrounding world of vital nature, cosmic
and animal, where a shining crupper of sky reminds us yet again,

---

[2] 'El coñac es una bebida para hombres que saben resistir' (II, 593).

amidst the confinement of the jail-house, of the escape that Antoñito did not attempt.

One important element in the poem has so far not been mentioned: the title. It is unusually long and explicit for a Lorca poem and one would like to to find an explanation. This is not difficult if one views the poem from the context of Andalusian popular culture. In Andalusia the word *prendimiento* ('taking', as opposed to 'arrest', *detención*) is almost uniquely associated with the taking of Christ and immediately suggests the corresponding *pasos* of the Holy Week processions: the Sagrado Prendimiento de Nuestro Señor Jesucristo in Seville, Nuestro Padre Jesús del Prendimiento in Malaga, and countless others. Antoñito, then, whom Lorca himself described as a 'gitano verdadero, incapaz del mal' (III, 345), is being tacitly compared to Christ in his meek submission to arrest. But resonances of the Passion do not end there, for the words *en el camino de Sevilla* seem clearly to echo the words 'en el camino del Calvario', traditionally used to refer to Christ's bearing of the Cross, and again Holy Week tableaux offer suggestive parallels (including the Calvary of the gypsy Jesús de la Salud in Seville), as also do a number of well-known paintings (most relevantly, perhaps, Raphael's *Caída en el camino del Calvario* in the Madrid Prado).[3] Antoñito, then, not only submits meekly; he also suffers from his submission (injustice of his enemies, incomprehension of his friends, loneliness in suffering). If my interpretation is correct, then, the title anticipates basic elements of the poem itself and, by echoing the Passion, serves both to ennoble and to universalise Antoñito's own calvary of misfortune. But it is not only the title. The *vara de mimbre* too may conceivably recall the Passion — and several Holy Week tableaux — where 'they put [. . .] a reed in his right hand' and mocked him as King of the Jews (Matthew 27:29); more certainly, the *cinco tricornios* (28), with a number that has mystified critics, recall the five civil guards who, when there is no resident military garrison or naval base, traditionally form the Holy Week escort for the tableau of Christ (one at each corner and the corporal behind), and the repeated *nueve de la noche* (39, 43) echoes the biblical 'ninth hour' when 'Jesus cried out with a loud voice, saying Eli, Eli, lama sabachthani? that is to say, My God, my God, why has thou forsaken me?' (Matthew 27:45–6). It may be relevant to recall also the *villancico* quoted by Josephs and

---

[3] The words *en el camino de Sevilla* were absent from the first published version of the poem (in *Litoral* 1, November 1926, 7–9), being added for the 1928 edition, presumably to make the reference clearer.

Caballero (264), in which *a la mitad del camino* is associated with the Christ child ('A la mitad del camino / viene el niño de Belén'). We shall find similar religious resonances in the following, companion poem. In footnote 1 I suggested that gypsy resonances serve to elevate Antoñito to archetypal gypsy and that resonances of ballad literature elevate him to archetypal hero. The echoing of biblical and Holy Week resonances, I now suggest, elevates him also to archetypal man of peace, 'incapaz del mal' (III, 345). Here as elsewhere, what matters in *Romancero gitano* is not the presence of such resonances — which has been tolerably documented — but the reason for their presence: in this case to enhance Antoñito by association, in the same way that Saint Gabriel and Anunciación were enhanced in the previous poem. We are touching on an aspect of Lorca's writing that has been strangely neglected.

Blanquat, in the most erudite study on the poem, finds 'un système d'allusions et de symboles que marque la volonté d'atteindre la tradition du paganisme antique et oriental avec celle du christianisme'; Umbral, mainly concerned with psychology, emphasises Lorca's *pansexualismo*; Feal Deibe finds much sexual symbolism that other readers may not find. Among the more straightforward textual readings, Correa finds elements of myth and DeLong supplements his findings; Petersen emphasises the poem's novelistic progression and the compression, resonances and interaction of its various elements; Durán Medina emphasises symbolic significance (of the sort pointed out by Flys, Eich and Ramos-Gil); A. Barroso and collaborators note the superposition of metaphor and imagery on the 'base narrativo-descriptiva' of the traditional Castilian *romance*; Cobb is somewhat discursive and Freud-infected; Lisboa keeps characteristically close to the text. In my own commentary I make the same points as in the above outline guide but with fuller evidence and debate.

Select bibliography: Correa, 40–1; J. Blanquat, 'Mithra et la *Rome andalouse* de FGL', in *RLC* 37 (1963), 337–49; F. Petersen, 'La vida corta pero eterna de Antonio el gitano', in *Hispanófila* 28 (September 1966), 39–47; Umbral, 113–15; B. J. DeLong, 'Mythic unity in Lorca's Camborio poems', in *Hispania* 52 (1969), 840–5; Feal Deibe, 205–13; Durán Medina, 95–8; A. Barroso and others, *Introducción a la literatura española a través de los textos*, Madrid 1983, 60–5; Cobb (1983), 85–7; Lisboa, 136–42; H. Ramsden, 'Lorca's "PAC ..."', in *Readings in Spanish and Portuguese Poetry for Geoffrey Connell*, ed. N. G. Round and D. G. Walters, University of Glasgow, 1985, 190–204.

12

MUERTE DE ANTOÑITO EL CAMBORIO

Antoñito is again the protagonist. The previous poem depicted his taking by the Civil Guard; the present one describes his death. It is not certain that his death is a direct consequence of his arrest in the previous poem, for narrative and causal links are characteristically muted. But there are at least pointers to this and I shall refer to them in my outline commentary. If my interpretation is correct the underlying suggestion of the poem is that among the various threats to the gypsy (the moon in Poem 1, the wind in Poem 2, the black angels of strife in Poem 3 ... and the Civil Guard in Poem 11) must be included also the exaggerated gypsy tradition of family honour. Because of this tradition the gentler, more magical and more estimable qualities of the gypsies are denied proper expression. For appreciation of the poem itself it matters little whether or not one accepts this suggestion; in other respects it merits consideration, both for its relevance to Lorca's basic theme of vitality and repression and as evidence of his growing awareness of honour as an element of repression (cf. *Bodas de sangre, Yerma, La casa de Bernarda Alba*).

1–4. There is an immediate evocation of a fight to the death, presumably at night, since the fight is identified by the shouts. Comparison with the opening lines of 'Reyerta' is revealing. In each case Lorca places the action specifically and significantly (*En la mitad del barranco; cerca del Guadalquivir*) but avoids a merely anecdotic approach and brings his reader straightaway to the heart of the conflict (in the earlier poem, the knives *bellas de sangre contraria*; in this poem, the *voces de muerte* which are then polarised into *voces antiguas* and *voz de clavel varonil*). This essentialising concentration is further helped by the epico-mythic resonances of *Albacete* and *Guadalquivir* respectively (cf. *Sevilla* in line 4 of 'Prendimiento ...'). But in the present poem the opening lines serve not only to bring the reader to the centre of the action. They also anticipate the fatal outcome and thereby impart a sense of inevitability that the earlier poem lacked. In context *antiguas* in *voces antiguas* suggests ancient gypsy lineage (cf. *viejos cuchillos* in the previous poem) but serves also as a contrast to the image of youthful vitality in *voz de clavel varonil*. One can, if one wishes, justify this interpretation of the latter words by reference to other places in Lorca's work where the carnation is associated with male passion and vitality (as opposed to the rose which is associated with young women), but the immediate context is sufficient.

5–18. The vitality of *clavel* is echoed and reinforced by the verb *clavó* (with its similar sounds) and is then developed in two striking animal images. The colour too reappears in Antoñito's red tie, now bathed in enemy blood (with a parallel to *sangre contraria* in 'Reyerta'), but they were four daggers (with a further echo of the metonymic *viejos cuchillos* of 'Prendimiento . . .') and he had to succumb (a more specific pointer to the outcome heralded in the title and opening lines). The pace of the poem is more rapid than elsewhere in *Romancero gitano*, with predominantly two-line periods, emphasis on verbal action and a sharply insistent *í* assonance. Then, in line 13, as in the previous poem (17–24), nature takes over the action, with a similar switch to the present tense to indicate withdrawal from anything resembling anecdote and a broadening of physical and emotive horizons. When the stars drive javelins into the water (a bullfighting image that recalls the previous poem and suggests the *puñales* of Antoñito's assailants), when yearlings are dreaming of *verónicas* of gillyflowers (a further bullfighting image, but now paralleling Antoñito's own gentleness), shouts of death resounded close to the Guadalquivir. One notes especially the build-up of tension created by the parallel subordinate clauses and the resolution of this tension in the final two lines which, with a return to the preterite, bring us back to the specific action and outcome presented in the opening lines of the poem.

19–40. The central section of the poem takes the form of a dialogue between the narrator and Antoñito. The narrator, initially, offers a build-up akin to that at the beginning of the previous poem: first the full resonant name (now restored after the denial of 11:29–34); then a reminder of the proud Camborio lineage (with a further suggestion of animal strength in *dura crin* and a pointer to the hero's firm profile); finally, two lines that we have seen already, one in the previous poem (line 5), the other in this poem (line 4). This use and repetition of key characterising elements is a well-known feature of epic narration (for example, the repeated reference to an epic hero as 'barba vellida', 'fardida lança', 'el que en buen ora çinxo espada', etc.) and contributes to the overall nobility of tone. Antoñito's life, then, is associated with desirable qualities. It is this that explains the special pathos of *¿Quién te ha quitado la vida?* (as opposed to the more commonplace and less expressive '¿Quién te ha matado?'), with a perfect tense to indicate that what was foretold has now virtually come about and with a reminder of the heralded place of death, *cerca del Guadalquivir*. Lest we were earlier tempted to assume, despite the *voces antiguas* of line 3 and the *puñales* of line 11, that Antoñito's assailants were the civil guards whom he refused to fight in the previous poem, his reply makes it clear: they were gypsy cousins worthy of the fight — from Benamejí (a magical name of Arabic origin, like so many Andalusian towns and villages; not far from Montilla, Poem 3, and Cabra, Poem 4, all in the province of Cordoba). Given the renowned closeness of gypsy family ties, normally disrupted only in cases of offence against family honour, it seems reasonable to assume that the four Heredia cousins are here taking revenge for the betrayal of their lineage revealed in the previous poem. By his apparent cowardice Antoñito has isolated himself from the Camborio clan (cf. *Si te llamaras Camborio* . . .; *Ni tú eres hijo de nadie, / ni legítimo Camborio*) and exposed himself to the revenge for which the *viejos cuchillos* were clamouring in 'Prendimiento . . .' (cf. the *voces antiguas* of the four cousins). But Antoñito, from his own standpoint of gentleness, cannot conceive of such a barbarously macho response and attributes the attack not to revenge for cowardice but to envy of his dandified elegance of maroon-coloured shoes, ivory pendants and delicate complexion.[1] The biblical echo seems clear, especially in view of the various resonances of the Passion of Christ noted in the previous poem: 'For he knew that for envy they had delivered him' (Matthew 27:18). It serves to reinforce and dignify Antoñito's own dislike of violence. The narrator is no longer deceived by appearances as he was in the 'Prendimiento . . .'. He now recognises

---

[1] In *color corinto* Lorca recalls one of the classic colours of the bullfighter's *traje de luces* (e.g. 'El torero iba de oro y corinto') and thereby complements the various other bullfighting references in the two Antoñito poems. He also draws on the duality of dandified elegance and death-defying valour commonly associated with the bullfighter. But Lorca's own special affection, it seems, was for the former; in his original poems and plays there are significantly more diminutive *torerillos* and *toreritos* than there are *toreros* (Alice M. Pollin, *A Concordance to the Plays and Poems of FGL*, Cornell UP, 1975, pp. 690, 1038).

his protagonist as the gentle, childlike person he is ('gitano verdadero, incapaz del mal', III, 345) and significantly addresses him with the diminutive *Antoñito*, used in both titles but not hitherto used within either poem: Antoñito, worthy of an Empress (with uplift akin to that noted in the description of the very similar gypsy Saint Gabriel in Poem 10, lines 11–14), remember the Virgin, for you are going to die. In his reply Antoñito addresses Lorca by his name ('el único de todo el libro que me llama por mi nombre en el momento de su muerte', III, 345), suggesting a special bond of affection based on temperamental affinities. Even the Civil Guard is now invoked in defence of his non-rebellious, non-aggressive way of life (a further betrayal of his gypsy ancestry and a reminder that the gypsy is virtually condemned by tradition to live in conflict with authority). But it is too late. The flexibility of Antoñito's *vara de mimbre* has gone. His slim figure has snapped like a stalk of maize.

41–52. The opening lines present the death, with *tres golpes de sangre*, Antoñito's proud *perfil* and a preterite to indicate completeness and distance. The *tres golpes de sangre* echo the *tres heridas* and *tres balas de almendra verde* of the Annunciation poem and the effect is reinforced by the already noted pointers to the Passion of Christ: the 'prendimiento', the variation on 'en el camino del Calvario', the passive acceptance of arrest, the biblical ninth hour, the envy-motivated death ... Antoñito is no longer merely a carefree, dandified gypsy. By biblical association he has become also an almost mythical man of peace condemned to die for his dislike of violence. It is an excellent example of how Lorca uses Christian resonances: to supplement his own characterisation and to universalise both his characters and the dilemmas that life forces upon them. Lines 43–4 take up the profile-proud death of the previous line with a tribute to Antoñito's unique profile-proud life and a suggested image of a victorious emperor coined in bronze (appropriate for one who has just been described as *digno de una Emperatriz*). As Saint Gabriel announced the coming birth in the Annunciation poem, so angels now watch over Antoñito in death, with the traditional oil-lamp and the cushion under his head. In the final lines, as the four cousins reached Benamejí, the voices of death that have echoed through the poem are silenced. The disrupted parallelism to lines 13–18, with *cesaron* replacing *sonaron*, serves to emphasise the contrast; the preterite, the finality.

The poem has been poorly served by critics. In the bibliography listed, Correa characteristically emphasises mythical resonances but believes that Antoñito's assailants are civil guards (which goes against much evidence in the poem and makes lines 23–6 and 38 wholly inexplicable); DeLong corrects Correa's misinterpretation, carries his mythical approach further and emphasises the unity of the two Antoñito poems; Umbral is content to elaborate at length on his notion of the poem's 'gran valor documental' since it is allegedly 'el máximo poema-invectiva al gran pecado nacional español, el pecado de la envidia' and can thus be seen as a premonition of Lorca's own death, also from envy; Loughran reaffirms a mythical approach with emphasis on cosmic involvement; Cobb's commentary is useful but not notably revealing; Lisboa offers the fullest commentary.

Select bibliography: Correa, 41–2; Umbral, 115–18; Beverly J. DeLong, 'Mythic unity in Lorca's Camborio poems', in *Hispania* 52 (1969), 840–5; Loughran (1978), 147–9; Cobb (1983), 87–9; Lisboa, 144–55.

13
MUERTO DE AMOR

First published in *Litoral* of Malaga, in a special *homenaje* number to
Góngora (5–7, October 1927), this is one of Lorca's most hauntingly
mysterious ballads. As in 'Romance sonámbulo', 'hay una gran sensación de anécdota, un agudo ambiente dramático y nadie sabe lo que
pasa' (III, 341). Together with 'Romance sonámbulo', writes Díaz-
Plaja, it is 'el ejemplo más típico de la inmersión del poeta en el mundo
superreal de las "fuerzas oscuras"'. On this at least there is agreement.
It is 'otro romance "sonámbulo" por sus calidades oníricas' (Umbral),
'one of Lorca's excursions beyond the limits of ordinary experience
into some sort of realm of his own imagining' (Campbell), 'hors des
limites de l'ordinaire; hallucinations, folie, destin caché' (Henry), 'aux
frontières du réel et de l'irréel [. . .], un univers fantastique' (Velasco).
But whereas in commentaries on 'Romance sonámbulo' there is a
general critical consensus on the underlying storyline, with few
divergent interpretations, on 'Muerto de amor' there is no such consensus. Thumbnail commentators tend to say nothing of the narrative,
referring only to the atmosphere of mystery and to the odd image in
isolation. Others disagree in their interpretation. Who, for example,
is the *muerto de amor*? Is he the son whose words open the poem
(Schonberg, Correa, Vázquez Ocaña, Henry, Belamich, Cobb, Ramos-
Gil, Josephs and Caballero, Velasco) or is he someone else (Andueza)? And if he is the son, is he already dying of love in the opening
lines (Vázquez Ocaña, Henry, Belamich, Cobb, Josephs and Caballero) or does his dying come only later, either by suicide (Schonberg,
Velasco) or because of involvement in a fight (Correa)? The greatness
of a Lorca *romance* lies less in its anecdote than in its 'sensación de
anécdota' and 'agudo ambiente dramático', but, as Lorca pointed out
in his lecture on Góngora, the anecdote, though it has no importance
in itself, 'da con su hilo invisible *unidad* al poema' (III, 243–4). In
'Muerto de amor', it has been suggested, the anecdotic thread is too
invisible. 'Perhaps the ballad suffers from a lack of narrative direction'
(Cobb). Certainly it is a poem 'de acción eludida o de plano real casi

escamoteado' (Ramos-Gil), with an 'hermétisme difficile à percer' (Velasco). But it produces an extraordinary sense of mystery and anguish. In the following pages I seek to explain at least some part of this.

1–8. A dialogue between mother and son. But as with similar opening dialogues in traditional *romances*, we are not immediately aware of this and the first two lines appear as an attention-seizing question to the reader and an invitation to mystery, with an indeterminate something that shines and *altos corredores* that could be simply corridors or walkways along the upper floor of a *corralón* or tenement building but seem in context to be more akin to the mythical *altas barandas* of 'Romance sonámbulo'.[1] The mystery is enhanced rather than dispelled by the mother's down-to-earth but evasive reply, and when the son is more specific about what he can see, with a pointer to four lamps that suggest a funeral wake, *sin querer* adds a sense of relentlessness that the mother's prosaic explanation again does nothing to dispel. She is either insensitive to the realm of mystery and misfortune glimpsed by her son or, more probably, as in the *RVC* examples quoted, is seeking to shield him from it. In either case her response serves to increase the mystery.

[1] Rizzo (in *Clavileño* 36, November–December 1955, 49) and Velasco quote three traditional poems that begin with the same first line. I here reproduce two of them:

¿Qué es aquello que reluce	¿Qué es aquello que reluce
por cima del Sacramento?	en aquel monte florido?
Será la Virgen María,	Es Jesús de Nazareno,
que va por agua a los cielos.	que con la cruz se ha caído.

All are taken from F. Rodríguez Marín's *Cantos populares españoles*, Seville 1882 (nos. 6381, 6382, 6524), a collection that Lorca certainly knew (Gibson, *FGL*, I, Barcelona 1985, p. 316). Since Lorca is presenting a dialogue between mother and child, the following lines too are relevant, especially since they are both from traditional *romances* that influenced *RG* 17:

Diga, diga la mi suegra;	Madre, la mi madre,
diga, diga suegra mía;	la mi siempre amiga,
¿por quién tocarán a muerto	pero ¿esas campanas
que las campanas tañían?	por quién las repican?
(*RVC* III, 111)	(*RVC* III, 178)

9–18.   These are among the finest lines in the poem, with a broadening of mystery and ill omen through the involvement of nature and a final return to the more specific nucleus of mystery and ill omen from which the poem started. The ominous note is developed initially in the image of the waning moon that drapes yellow hair over yellow towers. Possible romantic associations are dispelled by the metaphor of a clove of garlic and the waning is emphasised and given human relevance by the word *agónica*. Alvarez de Miranda's findings, referred to in my introductory comments on Poem 1, are again relevant: in primitive cultures the moon with its monthly cycle of birth, growth, decline and death is seen as an image of human life. Since the light it now casts is of dying silver, it can appropriately be described as yellow. Besides, to gypsies yellow is an inauspicious colour. Night, like beggar death (cf. *Bodas de sangre* III, i), taps trembling on the window-panes, pursued by *los mil / perros que no la conocen* (with an underlying reality that will be familiar to anyone who has approached an isolated Spanish village at night). In context, after the indicated train of ill omen, dying, pursuit and fear, the *corredores* to which we now return seem even more doom-laden. The smell of wine and ambergris, one feels, confirms one's earlier impression of a wake.

We can now take our stand, tentatively at least, on the critical disagreements indicated earlier. There are clear pointers to a wake and the son is fascinated by them. But there is no suggestion that he is dying and the mother's matter-of-fact *Cierra la puerta, hijo mío* suggests that he is active and mobile. The wake, then, must be explained either as someone else's wake or a visionary premonition of his own death. In a Lorcan context the hypothesis of a death foretold and then fulfilled is extremely tempting and the reader may well opt for this majority view. But the two *RVC* poems quoted in footnote 1 — both of which Lorca clearly knew — do not support it, for in each case the mother (or mother-in-law) seeks to shield a young person from the horror of someone else's death. More importantly, the overall internal evidence of 'Muerto de amor' seems to point in the same direction. The reader, for example, is made aware of the wake not as a premonition of the boy but directly through his own sense perceptions. And the title of the poem is not 'El muerto de amor' (or 'Romance del muerto de amor'), with an essentialising noun that would more easily allow for the death to take place within the poem, nor 'Muerte de amor', which would suggest that the death does take place within the poem, but 'Muerto de amor', with the suggestion of an already existing state.[2] If this is accepted — and since the son is clearly alive at the beginning — the *muerto de amor* would appear to be someone else. The difficulty of identifying that someone else might be the principal attraction of seeing the son as the *muerto de amor*. But this does not obviously accord with the evidence.

19–26. The first lines echo the previous poem, with breezes of *caña mojada* that contrast with the dried and broken *caña de maíz* of Antoñito's body (12:39–40) and *viejas voces* that recall the *voces antiguas* of his cousins (12:3). Their resounding through the broken arch of midnight has been seen as a chronological progression from *las once* (4) and this may well be so. But the associated resonances are more important, with a suggestion of disrupted harmony that parallels in sound (*resonaban por el arco roto*) the visual image of lines 1–2 (*reluce por los altos corredores*) and reinforces the earlier impression of ill omen and cosmic mystery. In context the sleeping oxen and roses suggest innocent unawareness of the tragedy. But Lorca was an enthusiast of early painting, and ox and broken arch are recurrent elements in early Nativities and Adorations.[3] Add to this the presence of roses, their traditional association with the Virgin Mary[4] and the poet's awareness of this ('Rosas, rosas, joyas vivas de infinito / [. . .] / tenéis en vuestro ser / una esencia divina: / María de Nazaret', I, 989–90), and the case seems clear: amidst the horror of death Lorca is evoking a contrasting image of the Nativity. Similar iconographic resonances were indicated in the immediately preceding Antoñito poems and both these poems, it was suggested, echo the earlier Annunciation poem, 'San Gabriel'. Since *caña mojada* (19) and *viejas voces* (20) also echo the Antoñito poems, one is impelled to infer that in 'Muerto de amor' there is a tacit allusion both to the death of Christ, the supreme *muerto de amor*,[5] and to the death of Antoñito. This does not of course

---

[2] Contrast Ramos-Gil's view: 'El título no ofrece dudas: se trata de un poemita de muerte en acto'. The reader will decide.

[3] See, for example, Hans Memling's Prado Adoration which has both. On the frequency and significance of crumbling edifices, see Barbara G. Lane, *The Altar and the Altarpiece*, New York 1984, p. 65.

[4] 'Rose. A flower particularly associated with the Virgin Mary who is called the "rose without thorns", i.e. sinless' (Hall *Dictionary* . . . , 330–1).

[5] With the temporal superposition of birth and death, as in 10:53 and 10:65–6 (see above, p. 69, especially footnote 4), but here with death as the real plane and the birth as the evoked plane.

assume a narrative link — any more than between Soledad's abandonment and that of the *casada infiel* —, but the echoes and resonances
seem indisputable. Nor can one overlook the fact that in the three traditional poems quoted by Rizzo and Velasco (above, p. 84) the
identical first line served to introduce either Christ or the Virgin. The
sceptic is invited to disagree with this interpretation, but he will have
much to explain that seems to have been neither noted nor explained:
the remarkable 'coincidence' of two echoes of 'Muerte de Antoñito el
Camborio' and three pointers to the Nativity — all within the space of
five lines (19–23) —, the relevant interaction of imagery and iconographic resonances in 'San Gabriel' and the Antoñito poems, and the
traditional religious resonances in line 1 of this poem. Also, presumably, he will need to offer a convincing alternative explanation of the
images in lines 19–23 as integrated elements in the poem's overall
progression. My case does not end at this point but, before proceeding
further, it is relevant to wonder why the above religious references are
so concealed that they have passed unnoticed: firstly, perhaps, because
Lorca wished to offer mere resonances rather than specific identification (something that we shall consider at greater length in the
commentary on *RG* 17); secondly, because he wished to obviate suggestions of blasphemy.[6] I return to textual commentary. After the
innocent sleeping of oxen and roses we are reminded, yet again (24–
6), of the inescapable horror of the wake by the four death-proclaiming
lights that now reappear with synaesthetic clamour.

27–42. The funeral procession and associated lamentation are presented in characteristic Lorcan terms, with a duality of repose in death
and bitter cutting short of youth, and with emphasis on the suffering
of the womenfolk who alone remain to accompany the body and to
lament their loss at this inescapable crisis moment of *cabelleras y
nombres* (an echo of line 11 and a suggestion, perhaps, of tearing the
hair and of naming the deceased and those responsible for the killing).
Given the already indicated iconographic resonances, it is tempting

---

[6] Compare the presentation of sexuality in 'La casada infiel' and 'Thamar
y Amnón' and Lorca's preference for the latter which, though 'mucho más
fuerte', is protected by its 'acento poético más difícil, que lo pone a salvo
de ese terrible ojo de guiña ante los actos inocentes y hermosos de la
Naturaleza' (III, 346). Since accusations of blasphemy have in fact been
made, though based on different evidence, Lorca was clearly justified in his
caution.

also to find in the weeping women *al pie del monte* an echo of the
biblical women at the foot of Calvary (cf. Van Eyck's Crucifixion and
many similar paintings) and to see the Christ/Antoñito, holy/profane
superposition further reflected in the juxtaposition of seraphims and
gypsies in line 37 (cf. 12:45–8).[7] The *fachadas de cal* (35), apart from
reflecting Andalusian reality, seem to impose order and structure on
the dark night of lamentation (cf. 14:54–8). Lines 39–42 pose a problem for those who see the son as the *muerto de amor* and presumably
have to be explained as a recollection of words spoken by him before
his death. Or lines 27–38 must be seen, as Ramos-Gil sees them, as
another visionary premonition. In my own proposed interpretation
there is no problem: the son continues merely as a fascinated observer
and, prompted by what he has seen, thinks of his own death, with an
echo of *cante* in *cuando yo me muera* (Josephs and Caballero, 273),
and wants it to be made known by blue telegrams (the traditional har-
bingers of misfortune for those who possess no phones) sent north and
south (uncontoured extent; cf. '¡Siempre la rosa, siempre, norte y sur
de nosotros!', I, 955). But the emotive impact of these lines (on the
present reader at least) suggests wider resonances, especially in view
of Lorca's emphasis on recitation and his frequent interventions as
narrator, with both dialogue (2:37–42, 7:9–38, 11:29–38, 12:33–6)
and comment (1:29–30, 4:1, 9, 13 ..., 15:17–24, 57–64, 117–24).
Aided by the exclamatory sense of *Madre*, it is as though, beyond the
boy's involvement, the narrator, overcome by the tragedy, intervenes
also on his own behalf. The progression from *ves* to *dejadme* in
'Romance sonámbulo' was not wholly dissimilar (above, comment on
4:47–50).

43–54. As several critics remind us, seven (43–4) is a magical number with many resonances. Josephs and Caballero quote a *siguiriya*
that includes the lines 'los siete dolores / que pasó mi Dios' and
Andueza, more relevantly, recalls the traditional seven sorrows of
the Virgin (commonly depicted as seven daggers in the heart, with red
flowers to represent the blood). As the *cantaor*'s anguished voice is re-
puted to shatter wine glasses, so cries of the womenfolk here shatter
mirrors, with consequent fragmentation of the reflection and associat-

---

[7] D. Harris makes similar points on these lines, indicating also that 'the
poppy [44] represents blood and death in Christian symbology' (in *BHS* 58,
1981, 331).

ed images of martyr-like mutilation (*manos cortadas*) and funeral wreaths. In the context of so many biblical resonances it may be relevant to recall also the rending of the veil of the temple at the death of Christ (Matthew 27:51) and I find it difficult not to associate *el mar de los juramentos* with Peter's repeated oaths and curses as he denied Christ (Matthew 26:72–5). Beyond the sea of oaths heaven itself was responding with a slamming of doors — desolation and abandonment?; 'My God, my God, why hast thou forsaken me?' (Matthew 27:46) — as the lights clamoured (with the widening and intensification of line 6) in the now clearly mythical high corridors.

I have indicated the main areas of critical agreement and disagreement and make no further comment.

Select bibliography: C. Ramos-Gil, *Claves líricas de GL*, Madrid 1967, pp. 281–7; Andueza, 66–70; J. Velasco, 'L'aspect narratif dans le *RG*: essai d'interprétation du romance "MA"', in *Mélanges à la Mémoire d'André Joucla-Ruau*, Aix-en-Provence 1978, II, 1205–17; Lisboa, 157–69.

14

ROMANCE DEL EMPLAZADO

An *emplazado* is one cited or summoned to appear within a certain time before a judge, in this case God. Lorca's *emplazado* has been warned that he will die within two months; at the end of two months the prophesy is fulfilled. The poem, then, tells of heralded misfortune and fatal outcome. It is one of Lorca's basic themes. It is also frequent in ballad literature. In the *Romancero del Cid*, for example, Saint Peter appears to the Cid and warns him, 'Morirás en treinta días, / desde hoy que esto te fablo', and then, like Lorca's Saint Gabriel, returns to heaven (*RC* 103). And in the 'Romance del conde Alarcos y de la infanta Solisa' the countess, as she is put to death, calls the king and infanta to judgment 'dentro de los treinta días' and her call is duly answered, for 'dentro de los treinta días / [...] / allá fueron a dar cuenta / a la justicia divina' (*RVC* 163). But Lorca's most immediate source, it seems, was the much narrated story of Ferdinand IV 'El Emplazado'. According to early *romances* the Carvajal brothers, Don Pedro and Don Alonso (or Don Juan or Don Rodrigo; the name of the second brother varies from version to version), were falsely accused of pillage and rape and were sentenced by the king to mutilation and death. At the moment of execution the younger brother appealed in vain against the sentence and besought God to summon the unrelenting king before Him within a period of thirty days. I quote two versions of the outcome:

El rey, no mirando en ello,
hizo complir su mandado
por la falsa información
que los villanos le habían dado;
y muertos los Carvajales,
que lo habían emplazado,
antes de los treinta días
él se fallara muy malo,
y desque fueron cumplidos,
en el postrer día del plazo,
fue muerto dentro en León,
do la sentencia hubo dado.

(*RVC* 64)

Y sin más poder decir
mueren estos hijosdalgo.
Antes de los treinta días
malo está el rey don Fernando,
el cuerpo cara oriente
y la candela en la mano.
Así falleció su Alteza,
de esta manera citado.

(*RVC* 64, n.)

Characteristically Lorca's *emplazado* has been democratised and freed from guilt: on the immediate plane he is a gypsy; on a universal plane he is Everyman.[1]

1–13. As in 'La casada infiel' the alternate-line assonance starts with the first line, as though a preceding line were missing. It serves to create space and silence around the exclamatory opening, to bring out the emotive resonances and to invoke the reader's attention for what follows.[2] Horse and rider are characteristically associated in anguish (with irruptive *Ojos chicos* and semantic and phonic contrasts suggesting agitation), unable to close their eyes at night or to give themselves up to the gentle voyage of sleep (with more lulling sounds, image and rhythm here, and an overall ralentando effect). But *Sino que* prevents more than a momentary involvement with the world of *sueño* and returns us abruptly to the sleepless world of the *emplazado*, with eyes clear, hard, ever on guard, fixed on the cruel fate that awaits him: *norte* (*course* but also *north*, with associated coldness), metals and crags (coldness and unyielding harshness), lifeless body (with maximum physical emphasis in the use of *sin venas* rather than *sin vida*) and frozen cards (further coldness and a reminder that the fate they foretell is rigid and unalterable). In an earlier commentary attention was drawn to the presence of similar images of fate and misfortune (3:5–8).

14–21. From the anguish of the protagonist there is an abrupt shift to an apparently detached and more relaxed scene, with boys bathing in a river. Lorca himself drew attention to the underlying popular image of powerful, slow-moving water as a *buey de agua* ('para indicar su volumen, su acometividad y su fuerza', III, 224) and here both literalises and develops the image, with plural *bueyes, embisten* and *cuernos* (the reflection of a crescent moon), to bring out the underlying animal association and to emphasise the 'acometividad y fuerza'. Inanimate nature (river), animal (ox) and cosmic element (moon), it seems, all conspire in the attack. What at first appeared as detached and relaxed now seems relevant to fate's onslaught on the *emplazado*.

---

[1] Another version of the same *romance* has been quoted by Cela (in *Primer viaje andaluz*) and reproduced by Josephs and Caballero (274). Lorca's poem first appeared in *Carmen* (Santander) 2, January 1928, 23–4.

[2] Compare the opening moments of *La casa de Bernarda Alba*: 'un gran silencio umbroso' broken only by the tolling funeral bells.

The following lines, with their connecting *Y*, make it clearer, for the relentless, *martinete*-like hammering on anvils, between sleeping and waking, brings us back to the sleeplessness of horse and rider. What started as a relaxation from immediate anguish is now seen as a means of broadening and universalising the implications of that anguish. Man, it seems, is subjected to forces that he cannot control.

22–41. The emphasis, so far, has been on anguish at the unstoppable force of fate. But no explanation has been given. In his lecture on Góngora's poetic imagery Lorca distinguished between the hard centre of an image (its 'núcleo central') and its wider resonances ('redonda perspectiva') (III, 230). There is a comparable duality here: lines 1–21 have emphasised the anguished 'redonda perspectiva'; in lines 22–41 the narrator intervenes with a flashback to the so far unidentified 'núcleo central'. On 25 June Amargo was warned to prepare for death. But 'prepare for death' is a colourless abstraction. Lorca's language, in contrast, is physical and immediate and is appropriately aided by a number of stylistic features that one associates with the traditional *romance*: the apparently factual, down-to-earth approach, the impressively natural word order, the emphasis on nouns and verbs (progression) rather than adjectives (description), the vivifying use of direct speech. All serve to encourage an immediate response in audience and reader. But in the greatest popular literature, while down-to-earth directness solicits our immediate attention, wider resonances (magic, mystery, fate ...) make a more subtle and more profound impact. It is something that Lorca exploits especially. The juxtaposition of precise date (22) and unspecified subject (23), for example, effectively associates the here-and-now with fate's impersonal and impassive decree; the name of the protagonist (here Amargo; *el emplazado* in the title) serves also to epitomise his destiny; the syntactical progression from invitation (24–5) to a repeated six-line interplay of admonition and decree (26–31, 36–41), with an intervening evocation of the appointed scene, appropriately at night (32–5), suggests the certainty of the outcome; key nouns, specific and physical, also have wider resonances of death (*adelfas, cruz, cicutas y ortigas, cal mojada* ...); personification suggests a conspiracy of death (*cicutas y ortigas / nacerán ...; agujas ... / te morderán*); mountains are magnetised as though indicating the unchangeable course of fate (32–4) and hard imagery serves to emphasise its harshness (38–9). In lines 40–1 this train of pointers to certain death is finally epitomised in another hard image, the anticipated laying out, and associated now with a specific time limit.

42–5. The reference to Saint James echoes the ballads of Ferdinand IV referred to earlier, for in summoning the king to appear before God within thirty days the younger Carvajal invoked Saint James as scribe and witness ('ponemos por escribano / al apóstol Santiago'). But Lorca has made the saint's presence in his own poem more obviously relevant, for Saint James's day is 25 July, the midpoint in Amargo's two-month calvary. Moreover, since Saint James is Spain's patron saint, his presence, together with his nebular sword (another cosmic element, probably associated with the Milky Way, popularly known as the 'vía de Santiago') serves to mythicise further Amargo's individual fate. Even the sky — heaven too — responds to his plight with turned back and cosmic silence.

46–57. The poem's conclusion is the more moving because of its impressive emotional austerity: the contrasted opening and closing of eyes that epitomises the beginning and end of Amargo's Calvary; the stoic contemplation of death (with lines that anticipate Lorca's call for men alone to behold the dead Ignacio Sánchez Mejías);[3] the final attainment of rest (*con descanso* in contrast to the opening *sin descanso*) but with the recognition of man's persistent *soledad*; the finding in death of a serene dignity of profile and sculpted form that life, with its tensions and torments, threatens constantly. 'Un muerto en España,' said Lorca, 'está más vivo como muerto que en ningún sitio del mundo: hiere su perfil como el filo de una navaja barbera' (III, 312). For Lorca, it seems, the gypsy is not only the epitome of 'lo más elevado, lo más profundo, más aristocrático' of Andalusia and 'lo más representativo de su modo' (III, 340); he is also the incarnation of what the poet finds most noble and profound in Spaniards as a whole — and perhaps in Everyman. The contrast with writers of the 98 Generation, who based their very different generalisations on Castilian country people, has a personal, artistic and generational significance that has still to be explored.

Critical commentary on this poem is generally sparse. González-Cruz's is the most comprehensive; Blanquat's the most erudite, with pointers to echoes of ancient literature and Roman religions.

Select bibliography: Henry, 231–3; Blanquat, 389–92; Loughran (1978), 162–3; L. F. González-Cruz, 'Muertes del Amargo: el "RE"', in *GLR* 7 (1979), 25–35; Cobb (1983), 91–3; Lisboa, 171–83.

[3] Yo quiero ver aquí los hombres de voz dura.
   Los que doman caballos y dominan los ríos (I, 557).

15

ROMANCE DE LA GUARDIA CIVIL ESPAÑOLA

For Lorca the gypsy's world is under constant threat: the death-bringing moon (Poem 1), the erotic pursuing wind (Poem 2), black angels of discord (Poem 3) .... The main part of *Romancero gitano* concludes with a mini epic in which their world is destroyed entirely: by their traditional real-life enemies, the Civil Guard. On the one hand the Civil Guard is popularly seen in Spain as the most disciplined and incorruptible of the country's forces of law and order; on the other they are associated with over-rigorous methods, especially in the treatment of those involved in petty crime. Lorca referred to the latter point in a letter to his brother, probably written in February 1926:

> El país [las Alpujarras] está gobernado por la guardia civil. Un cabo de Carataunas, a quien molestaban los gitanos, para hacer que se fueran los llamó al cuartel y con las tenazas de la lumbre les arrancó un diente a cada uno diciéndoles: 'Si mañana estáis aquí *caerá otro*.' Naturalmente los pobres gitanos mellados tuvieron que emigrar a otro sitio. Esta Pascua en Cáñar un gitanillo de *catorce años* robó cinco gallinas al alcalde. La guardia civil le ató un madero a los brazos y lo pasearon por todas las calles del pueblo, dándole fuertes correazos y obligándole a cantar en alta voz. Me lo contó un niño que vio pasar la comitiva desde la escuela. Su relato tenía un agrio realismo conmovedor. Todo esto es de una crueldad insospechada ... y de un fuerte sabor *fernandino* (cit. Hernández, 173).

In the ballad of the Civil Guard the ostensible gypsy narrator naturally takes a similar view. But persecution is also a basic theme of *cante*. According to Lorca his poem was started towards the end of 1924 and taken up again in November 1926, at which stage he sent Guillén the first 62 lines and outlined his intentions for the rest (III, 899–901). 'Las escenas del saqueo serán preciosas,' he commented. 'A veces, sin que se sepa por qué, [los guardias civiles] se convertirán en centuriones romanos. Este romance será larguísimo, pero de los mejores.' In fact the poem did not develop as intended, but it is worth noting both the author's enthusiasm and his pointer to mythicising transposition. For some readers this *romance* is the high point of the book.

1–16. The approach of the Civil Guard. But the title dispenses with the need to name them directly and Lorca's emphasis is on associated emotive resonances: the insistent blackness of horses and horseshoes; the metonymic capes, with scornful pointers to bureaucratic oppression (*tinta*) and religious ceremonial (*cera*); the leaden skulls that make them incapable of feeling; their patent leather souls, with transference from the classic *tricornio* to suggest further insensitivity .... At each stage a specific physical reference suggests something wider and more ominous. Hunched (with knapsacks under their capes that point also to deformed beings) and nocturnal (operating at night but with corresponding emotive darkness), they instil fear with their silent passing (further darkness in *oscura* and a fine image of fearful yielding to them in the image of grains of sand that give way beneath their tread). The passage concludes with the scornful dismissal even of their proclaimed military skills.[1]

17–24. A contrasting evocation of the gypsy town, with an exclamatory first line that sets up resonances of yearning that will continue through the rest of the poem, and a second line that echoes similar *cante* lines and points to festive celebration.[2] Unlike the dark world of the civil guards, that of the gypsies is characterised by natural elements strangely juxtaposed to suggest a child's fairy-tale realm of magic in which the gingerbread house of *Hansel and Gretel* would not be out of place. But line 22, with past tense and *recuerda*, introduces a note of nostalgia that both intensifies and makes more forlorn the yearning of the preceding line, and the bitter-sweet note continues in lines 23–4.

25–36. The night scene of the previous section was suggested not by darkness (too akin to the Civil Guard) but by light (the moon). Now, with the contrast established, Lorca can resume his narration. As night was approaching, the gypsies were forging suns and arrows. The darker

---

[1] For a fuller examination of the interplay of physical reference and wider resonances, see Carlos Bousoño's twelve-page commentary on line 9 (*Teoría de la expresión poética*, II, 430–42).

[2]   Esta noche vi a poner
      en las esquinas banderas.

(cit. José Mora Guarnido, *FGL y su mundo*, Buenos Aires 1958, p. 190). Josephs and Caballero quote also a relevant gypsy *cante festivo*: 'Qué bonito está Triana / cuando le ponen al puente / las banderitas gitanas' (280).

resonances of line 25, with their continuing pointer to the Civil Guard (especially in view of the imperfect tense), are playfully brushed aside by the magical *noche que noche nochera* (with an echo of the *luna lunera* of children's rhymes), but the contrasting presence of the gypsies as forgers of light is surely not fortuitous. Espejo-Saavedra has noted the influence of lines from Salvador Rueda in which the arrows are clearly the sun's rays ('ya el sol viene clavando / sus flechas de oro en la niebla'), and Lorca has characteristically compressed the image to suggest both a gypsy craft and mythical status (Vulcan's forge). Beyond the approach of night there is a further ominous note in the image of the wounded horse that beats on every door and the effect of the crowing *gallos de vidrio* (both stylised and suggestive of piercing cry) is not wholly dissimilar. The personified wind is surprised in its nakedness (superb lines that I am unable to explain logically) *en la noche platinoche, / noche que noche nochera* (further magic of word music and another moon-like contrast to the Civil-Guard night of *goma oscura*).

37–56.   As in 'San Gabriel' Lorca here elaborates on the way in which religious figures are viewed by the gypsies not as historically remote but in terms of their own real-life experience. The Virgin and Saint Joseph especially are considered attentive to gypsy children,[3] and the notion that they have lost their castanets and look to the gypsies for help in finding them is particularly delightful. Thereafter Lorca creates, as though for a puppet theatre, a nativity scene of the sort that Spanish children prepare every year: the Virgin attired with all the splendour of a mayor's wife, in silver paper, with a necklace of almonds, and Saint Joseph in a silken cape. And what more natural, for the Andalusian gypsy, than that the three wise men should be accompanied by the king of sherry (especially since we are in Jerez de la Frontera)? The moon, presumably seen low over a bell-tower where storks nest, is associated with the stork in an ecstasy of dream amidst further pointers to festive celebration. But there is nostalgia, too, in the image of dancers sobbing for their lost figures at this time of festivity, and the

[3]   La Virgen y San José
       escuchan con atención
       a los gitanitos morenos
       y les dan su bendición.

(Juan de Dios Ramírez Heredia, *Nosotros los gitanos*, Barcelona 1972, pp. 96–7).

duality is taken up in the incantatory *agua y sombra, sombra y agua* of the closing lines.

57–64. The yearning and nostalgia reappear with the repetition of earlier lines and are associated now with the approach of the Civil Guard (and a slightly ironic reminder of their official title, 'la benemérita [institución]'). The town must put out its lights. Like the *bailarinas sin caderas* it too is now ill-prepared for festive celebration.

65–72. The contrast between civil guards and gypsy town is succinctly suggested in the opening lines: on the one hand the relentless disciplined progression (with firm rhythm, dark nasal resonances and repeated stressed *o*); on the other hand the festive town (with a line remarkable for its agility and range of vowel sounds). Amidst murmuring flowers of remembrance ('Siempreviva de la muerte, / flor de las manos cruzadas', II, 936) and the double night of cloth (a pointer to the double column of course, with a further reminder of the guards' inhumanity since they are again characterised by their uniform rather than by human attributes) the relentless line 65 reappears. As in 14–16 the final note is one of scorn: their astronomy that knows only of pistols is now complemented by a sky (and heaven) that for them is a mere shop window of spurs.

73–116. There is another contrast in the first four lines: between the unsuspecting gypsy city and the attacking civil guards. The clocks stopped (with an effect on the reader akin to Lorca's relating of human affairs to cosmic events) and the brandy, commonly associated with heat and passion, disguised itself as cold November in order not to cause suspicion. The earlier crowing cocks are recalled in the agonised cry from weather vanes, as breezes (nature in its freedom and vitality) are cut and trampled. Along streets of half light old gypsy women flee with sleepy horses and money boxes.[4] Up steep streets dark capes

---

[4] I find an echo here of a well-known traditional *romance* on the siege of Alora:

> Viérades moros y moras
> todos huir al castillo;
> las moras llevaban ropa,
> los moros harina y trigo,
> y las moras de quince años
> llevaban el oro fino,
> y los moricos pequeños
> llevaban la pasa e higo (*RVC* 79).

(with further dehumanising metonymy) leave behind them flurries of scissors (a pointer to a characteristic gypsy occupation). In the doorway of Bethlehem (but also *crèche, Nativity tableau*; an echo of lines 41–8) Saint Joseph shrouds a young girl and the Virgin tends the children with spittle of stars (an echo of gypsy spells; cf. 7:35–6). But (a key word in Lorcan narrative) the Civil Guard advances sowing fires of destruction where imagination, young and naked, burns. The image is prompted by the context of burning and persecution and critics may well be right in seeing imagination itself personified as a martyr. But the associated emphasis on the destruction of imagination by the forces of order seems more doubtful, for *se quema* here suggests not so much destruction as ardour (i.e. the imagination is ablaze with the horrors of the scene; cf. identical usage in 'mi recuerdo se quema', I, 553). The imagination, then, rises phoenix-like from the burning, with a typically Lorcan juxtaposition of contradictory resonances, a heralding of the final lines of the poem and a pointer to the theme of martyrdom and resurrection in the next poem. There is another pointer to the next poem in the description of Rosa and her martyr-like mutilation (see below, commentary on 16:49–50). As other girls fled with their braids trailing behind them (but personified to suggest involvement in the pursuit), stylised gun flashes fill the air. When the town had been razed to the ground, the dawn appeared over the horizon like a cosmic giant.

117–24. Amidst flames of destruction the civil guards' departure, ominously silent like their arrival, is interwoven with the repetition of earlier lines of yearning and nostalgia. Because of their present context they echo even more forlornly than before. The gypsy city is now merely a memory, to be sought in the magical interplay of moon and sand in the poet's mind. But memory in the poet's mind is also, potentially at least, the work of art. In his final lines Lorca indicates the point from which *Romancero gitano* started.

Lisboa's is the most substantial commentary on the poem, but those by Díaz-Plaja, Correa, Loughran and Cobb are similarly text-based and helpful. Umbral emphasises political relevance and alleged premonition of the Spanish Civil War. Espejo-Saavedra points to the influence of Salvador Rueda on certain details of the poem and considers the stylistic difference.

Select bibliography: Díaz-Plaja, 129–33; Correa, 44–5; Umbral, 119–23; Loughran (1978), 149–53; R. Espejo-Saavedra, 'Una fuente del "RGCE" de FGL', in *RoN* 19 (1978–79), 172–6; Cobb (1983), 93–6; Lisboa, 186–206.

16
MARTIRIO DE SANTA OLALLA

Intro.

Romancero gitano concludes with three 'romances históricos' that stand somewhat apart from the rest of the book and are among the most difficult and least satisfactorily studied. The first evokes the martyrdom of the young Saint Eulalia of Merida, probably in AD 304. But the first gypsies entered Spain more than eleven hundred years after this and the original title, 'Romance del martirio de la gitana Santa Olalla de Mérida' (III, 901), suggests that Lorca, characteristically ahistoricist, was seeking both to integrate the martyrdom into his gypsy ballad book and to elevate his gypsy by association with a popular saint. In the definitive title he muted the anachronism by eliminating the explicit gypsy reference, but maintained the association more tacitly, aided by a popular form of the saint's name, by the *Romancero gitano* context in which the poem appears and by the similar tone and character of poem and book. It is possible too that he was influenced by a popular source (Díaz-Plaja) but none has so far been identified and, in the light of Scobie's study especially, it seems fairly sure that his main source was the Latin hymn to Saint Eulalia by the Hispano-Roman poet Prudentius (348–410).[1]

In the first 130 lines of the 215–line Latin poem the twelve-year-old Eulalia appears with all the self-righteousness and insolent fanaticism of a fourth-century terrorist: precociously earnest character (1–35), indignation at the treatment of Christians and escape from the seclusion in which a concerned mother tried to keep her (26–65), goading of the governor of Merida by insults of him, the emperor and their gods (66–95), response to the governor's tolerant, almost fatherly warning and advice by spitting in his eyes and scattering his holy images (96–130). There is none of this robust Christianity in Lorca's poem. Nor is there any of Eulalia's exultation in suffering (interspersed through lines

---

[1] Since no Castilian version appears to have been published until 1943 (*Peristephanon*, trans. M. J. Bayo), Lorca may well have consulted Costa y Llobera's 1924 Catalan translation. In what follows above I shall quote, where necessary, from H. J. Thomson's English version, included in his Loeb Classics edition of Prudentius (London 1953, II, 142–57).

131–60). Lorca's emphasis is on the horror of the martyrdom (II; cf. Prudentius 131–60) and on what follows (III; cf. 161–215). But he also has a remarkable opening section, wholly absent from Prudentius, in which he evokes Merida, the capital of Roman Lusitania, the scene of the martyrdom and the site, today, of some of Spain's most impressive Roman remains.

1–12. The long-tailed horse has been seen as both river (Campbell) and breeze (Loughran). Neither assumption seems necessary and I am myself inclined to emphasise the obvious echo of the mythical *caballo malherido* in the previous poem and to find a similar pointer to impending danger, in contrast to the soldiers who simply dice or doze in careless insensitivity. In a pre-publication draft (*A* I, 173) Lorca first wrote *juegan a los dados* (3). Apart from confirming my suggested *dice*, this makes clear a reference to countless early paintings of the Crucifixion in which soldiers are depicted throwing dice for Christ's garments (cf. Matthew 27:35). But Lorca then changed the line to *juegan y dormitan*, 'Por parecerle superflua la concreción', suggests García Posada. I sense more positive reasons: an increased effect of human insensitivity to the imminent martyrdom (in contrast to the prancing horse of ill omen) and a deliberate echoing of another biblical episode much represented in early painting, Christ's agony in the garden (cf. *Al gemir la santa niña*, 18) contrasted with the insensitive sleeping of the disciples (Matthew 26:36–46). The effect of these echoes of the Passion of Christ is to ennoble Olalla's martyrdom and to enhance its significance. I find a similar broadening of significance in the ensuing description of Merida. Lines 5–6 in particular are remarkably compressed. The *Minervas* are usually interpreted as olive trees (the tree of Minerva; Loughran, García Posada) or shrubs (regional usage; Flys). But Minerva was also the goddess of wisdom, a goddess of war and one of the great triad of Roman state divinities. The *medio monte de Minervas*, then, suggests not only trees but also a profusion of statues that recall the spiritual and martial vitality of Rome. But the vitality now has gone, for the arms of the statues, unlike those of the Daphne myth, are *sin hojas*, akin to the limbless statues of present-day Merida. There is thus a multiple superposition of references: statues/trees, Minerva/Daphne, Roman Merida/modern Merida, Roman greatness/Roman decline.[2] The impression of lost

_____

[2] Flys has cited these lines — also lines 9–12 — as an example of 'superposición significacional', noting 'dos significados totalmente diver-

vitality is further reinforced by the suspended water, which I take
to be frozen, possibly as snow, along the crests of the rocks (7–8),
and mutilation reappears in the night of recumbent torsos (prostrate
soldiers and limbless statues; a further superposition suggestive of lost
energies, especially in view of the funereal *yacentes*) and broken-nose
stars (a cosmic echoing of Merida's mutilated statues and, more
widely, of Rome's own battered glory) (9–10). This symbolic dark
night of ruin awaits its final destruction with the coming of a new dawn
(11–12).

13–22. The silence is broken by a series of sounds that serve as a
gradual transition to the awaited dawn and martyrdom: the occasional
crowing of cocks (13–14), with a transferred epithet, the red of the
comb being applied to the crowing, which I take to be blasphemous
not only 'por perturbador del silencio y reposo de cuantos duermen'
(García Posada) but as an echo of the cockcrows that confirmed Peter's
denial of Christ (Matthew 26:74–5);[3] the moaning of the holy girl
which, like the singing of a *cantaor*, shatters wineglasses (15–16) and
reminds us of the awaited *grietas del alba* through which the Roman
night will be shattered; the sharpening of knives and hooks for the
coming torture (17–18). As the bull of the anvil bellows (a fine image
of power and anguish that suggests also the forging of instruments
of torture) Merida puts on the crown of approaching day, with a mingling of white flowers, *casi despiertos*, and more ominous brambles (a
pointer, perhaps, to the biblical crown of thorns; agony and awaited
rebirth).

23–50. I have difficulty with lines 23–4 and know of no satisfactory
explanation. The manuscript probably offers the necessary clues, for
lines 23–4 and 25–6 were originally inverted and the present line 23
(then 25) read *Flora desnuda sonríe* (then *se aleja*, then *se evade*, then
se sube). Lines 27ff thus followed on originally from the presentation
of Flora, and the pronoun *le* (28) and possessive *Su* (29) referred to
her. The Roman goddess of flowers and spring, then, appeared as an

sos', but has been criticised by García Posada, who finds no allusion to the
decadence of Rome. If my own interpretation is correct there are even
more levels of meaning than those noted by Flys.

[3] Note, however, Campbell's commonly accepted but perhaps less
appropriate interpretation: 'a centurion rising in the light of a camp-fire
with his red-plumed helmet and issuing an order with curses'.

image of Olalla whose torment was being described. But on the evoked
plane spring's smiling response to the already presented horror of a
tray for cut breasts must have seemed inappropriate and gave way to
escape from horror (*se aleja, se evade*). But this, in turn, was inappropriate to Olalla and Lorca, presumably, then reordered lines 23–6 as
at present and, since the horror of cut-off breasts now followed, changed *se evade* to *se sube*. Flora thus appears finally not as an image of
Olalla but as an indication of relevant setting: approaching spring, akin
to the heralded dawn (11, 20–2), but still distant, since Flora is so far
desnuda. But what are the *escalerillas de agua*? There are 'escaleras de
agua' in the Generalife in Granada but I find no relevance in them to
this poem. Nor do I see them as Olalla's tears (García Posada). Perhaps my earlier interpretation of *agua en vilo* as frozen water is relevant. Lorca is after all describing a winter scene (as is seen more
clearly later) and if one moves up ladders of water this water too must
be frozen. There thus appears to be a visionary juxtaposition of contrasting elements: on the one hand the inert, comatose civilisation of
Rome; on the other hand the promise of spring, an appropriate setting
for the new life heralded by Olalla's martyrdom. Evidence on the latter
point is so far slim but is strengthened by later elements in the poem,
initially by the description of the martyrdom itself in which gushing
veins (27), streams of milk (38) and a thousand trickles of blood (39)
serve, as it were, to unfreeze the scene so far presented and are accompanied by pointers to dynamism in conflict with restriction: Olalla's sex
which trembles like a bird ensnared (29–30) and her hands, *ya sin
norma*, which leap and cross themselves in defiance of the double
mutilation of *manos cortadas* and *oración decapitada* (31–4) — and of
the more general mutilation by which Merida itself has been characterised.[4] Even the *arbolillos de sangre* are presented as a form of defiance (*oponen*) and the diminutive heavens and streams of milk seem
to herald a new and more fecund faith. The relevance of two of the
most important life symbols in Christian art seems obvious: Christ's
blood and the Virgin's milk. The flesh of the centurions (apparently

---

[4] Prudentius described 'the grace of [Eulalia's] maidenhood [shielded]
behind the covering of her head [her long flowing hair]'. Lorca, responding
to the suffering involved, has associated the 'covering of her head' with
Merida's crown of thorns and converted mere shielding into a characteristic image of ensnared vitality (29–30; cf. 5:5–6). There is nothing in
Prudentius corresponding to lines 31–4 but, as Scobie has pointed out, the
image of a severed hand appears elsewhere in Lorca's work: in poem
(above, 13:47), prose (III, 253, 482) and drawing (III, 1041).

yellow and grey at the same time; ominous emotive colouring), if not
reborn, is at least *desvelada*, stirred from the lethargy of *dormitan* and
torsos yacentes, with a possible echo of Prudentius's executioner who
'amazed and confounded broke away and fled from what his hands had
done' (173–4) and a more probable echoing of the biblical Passion:
'Now when the centurion saw what was done, he glorified God' (Luke
23:47). Lines 45–6 would thus suggest a remorseful clamouring at the
gates of heaven.[5] Meanwhile, amidst the clamour, the order implicit in
lines 25–6 has been carried out and the Consul bears Olalla's breasts
on a tray, with an echo of countless paintings of martyrdoms and a
similar mingling of horror and stylisation.[6]

51–66. 'Suddenly [after the burning] the icy winter pours down snow
and covers all the square, covering Eulalia's body too where it lies
under the cold sky, like a linen shroud [. . .]. The very elements at
God's command are performing thy obsequies, O maiden' (Pruden-

----

[5] The difficulty of these lines is usually passed over without comment.
In the studies listed only Loughran, Lisboa and García Posada attempt
to elucidate: Loughran and Lisboa by reference to real-life climatic phen-
omena (e.g. 'Clearly, there are no "yellow centurions" going off into the
sky, but rather clouds colored by the rising sun that keep watch over the
event like the angels of the "Death of Antoñito" and "Vendetta" ', Loughran); García Posada with a suggestion that the soldiers 'forman parte del
cortejo que acompaña el alma de Olalla al paraíso'. Though not wholly
convinced by any of these interpretations, I find myself closest to García
Posada with his more visionary, less realistic interpretation of the image.

[6] Prudentius offers a possible starting-point: 'In a moment [as an immediate response to Olalla's upturning of the governor's sacrifice to the
gods] two executioners are tearing her slim breast, the claw [cf. *garfios*, 18]
striking her two girlish sides and cutting to the bone' (131–4). But early
paintings offer closer parallels: John the Baptist's head on a tray, Saint
Lucy's eyes on a tray and, especially, Saint Agatha's breasts on a tray:
'Among the barbarities to which St Agatha was said to have been subjected was the cutting off of her breasts, and she is often represented in art
carrying them on a dish' (*The Penguin Dictionary of Saints*, p. 34). Azorín,
in his *Lecturas españolas* (1912), describes a painting of Saint Casilda that
is also close to Lorca: 'La santa está representada con los pechos cortados;
en la blancura nítida del seno se destacan dos redondeles color de sangre.
Al pie de un árbol reposan, en una bandeja de plata, los dos pechos
tajados' (Azorín, *OC* II, 606). It may also be that, here as elsewhere in the
poem, Lorca was influenced by a so far unidentified painting of Eulalia's
own martyrdom.

tius, 176–85). It is this that Lorca develops in the third part of his triptych, but in successive stages: first with contrast between the background whiteness of fallen snow and the blackness of Olalla's body, night's inkwells and tailors' dummies (mutilation again of course — and surrealist imagery —, with an echo of Olalla's own earlier *gemir*); then, after a further downfall of snow, the whiteness of Olalla's body, with a shift (from 52, 56) to *Olalla blanca en el árbol*. In 65–6 I find another echo of the Passion of Christ (the lance in the side) and a possible suggestion of metallic vultures (since *picos* are also *beaks*) where earlier there was the mere threat of blaspheming cockcrows.

67–74. Light bursts in upon the new day in the form of a monstrance against the burnt skies. The frozen *agua en vilo* and *escaleras de agua* have been released by the vitalising effect of the *chorro de venas verdes* that sprang from Olalla's throat (*garganta*) and now appear as free-flowing *gargantas de arroyo* (stream gorges), earlier images of leafless arms and ensnared birds yield to contrasting *ruiseñores en ramos* (70), and the static, sterile whiteness of winter (and of Roman civilisation) gives way to leaping, bursting *vidrios de colores* (71) suggestive of both spring and apotheosis. Comparison with Prudentius is revealing. Whereas the Latin poet finally distanced himself in time from the event to describe the saint's tomb and its location ('Overhead the gleaming roof flashes light from its gilded panels, and shaped stones diversify the floor so that it seems like a rose-covered meadow blushing with varied blooms', 196–200) and to invite homage ('the cold is tempered and loosens its grip on the land to load our basket with flowers [for tribute]', 204–5) Lorca presents the new spring as a consequence of the martyrdom. In the closing lines the elevation and mythicisation of Olalla's martyrdom is finally confirmed by fusion with Catholic liturgy and direct quotation from it.[7]

---

[7] The most relevant version of the liturgy known to me is the following, quoted by Quintiliano Saldaña to illustrate religious resonances in Ganivet's *El escultor de su alma*:

> arcángeles, querubines
> ángeles y serafines
> dicen, santo, santo, santo.
>
> (*Angel Ganivet*, Madrid 1930, p. 181)

[contd.]

In the commentaries listed Lunardi finds influence of Dante but is opposed by Díaz-Plaja and Bayo who emphasise Prudentius and hagiographic tradition; Correa is brief but perceptive; Scobie considers various possible sources, demonstrates the importance of Prudentius and makes some good observations; Loughran has published two commentaries, with emphasis on the work's necessary ambiguity of 'macro- and microcosmic' interpretation; Cobb finds Freudian significance but is not at his best on this poem; Lisboa's commentary is characteristically long and detailed; García Posada's study is one of the most comprehensive published on any Lorcan *romance*. On the poem's overall progression Lunardi finds, beyond Lorca's subtitles, a gradation of colour and light, from night to the cold light of dawn and on to the 'luz alta e irisada del Paraíso', an interpretation that later critics, in so far as they consider progression, accept or merely refine. I am alone, I think, in suggesting that Olalla's martyrdom itself underlies and prompts this progression, with the bringing of a new dawn, a new spring and a new vitality to the comatose and sterile civilisation of Rome evoked in Part I of the poem. Alone, too, in my emphasis on echoes of both Bible and Christian iconography — though Loughran refers to one of my examples, the lance in the side — and on their enhancing effect on Olalla's martyrdom. It is not certain that all critics will accept this interpretation. The reader is invited to be critical.

Select bibliography: G. G. Lunardi, 'Sobre el "MSO" ', in *Entregas de Poesía* (Barcelona) 21 (1946), n.p.; Díaz-Plaja, 133–5; M. J. Bayo, 'Sobre el "Romance de SO" de FGL', in *Clavileño* 13 (January–February 1952), 20–4; Correa, 45–6; A. Scobie, 'Lorca and Eulalia', in *Arcadia* 9 (1974), 290–8; Loughran (1978), 153–7 (with an earlier version in 'Myth, the gypsy and two "romances históricos" ', *MLN* 87, 1972, 253–71); M. García Posada, 'Un romance mítico: el "MSO", de GL', in *Revista de Bachillerato* 8 (October–December 1978), Cuaderno monográfico 2, 51–62; Cobb (1983), 96–9; Lisboa, 209–22.

Don Alfonso de la Fuente Adónez, the librarian of the Seminario Conciliar in Madrid, has suggested to me that this was probably from a local Andalusian version of the Preface of the Mass. Cf. 'Quam laudant Angeli atque Archangeli, Cherubim quoque ac Seraphim, qui non cessant clamare quotidie, una voce dicentes: Sanctus, Sanctus, Sanctus.'

17

BURLA DE DON PEDRO A CABALLO
(ROMANCE CON LAGUNAS)

Though apparently simple in language, this poem is one of the most difficult in the book and has prompted widely different interpretations. The first draft, entitled 'Romance con lagunas', is dated 28 December 1921 (that is, 'Día de Inocentes', the nearest Spanish equivalent to April Fool's Day) and Lorca presumably saw this as significant, for he retained the date in the revised version that, six years later, he sent for publication in *Mediodía* of Seville ('28 de diciembre 1921–1927'; Hernández, 165). In the definitive version he omitted the date but incorporated the *burla* into the title. This *burla*, it seems, is directed not only at Don Pedro but also at the reader and critic; initially by the form of the poem, allegedly a *romance* but with a notable variety of line-lengths (from 3 to 11 syllables) and with departure, at moments, even from alternate-line assonance; then, more significantly, in the poem's three *lagunas*. In what follows I shall be as brief as possible in my own survey and thereafter devote greater space than usual to the findings and hypotheses of others.

1–12. The opening indication of place, action and protagonist (with popular resonances in the direct style, the traditional *vereda* and the *romance*-echoing Don Pedro) is immediately broadened in significance by the exclamatory, emotive lines 3–4.[1] There is further broadening in the following lines, with the initially neutral *venía* now accompanied by

[1] As in traditional *romances* so also in Lorca's it is often difficult to distinguish between general resonance and specific influence. The following three *romances* (one on Peter the Cruel; the other two apparently of French or Germanic origin, *RVC* III, 112–15, 178) could conceivably suggest both. I here quote only the opening lines:

1. Por los campos de Jerez
   a caza va el rey don Pedro;
   allegóse a una laguna,
   allí quiso ver un vuelo.
   (*RVC* 66a)

2. Ya viene Don Pedro
   de la guerra herido;
   viene con el ansia
   de ver a su hijo (*RVC* III, 177).

[contd.]

an unbridled horse (with a fine galloping effect in the amphibrach rhythm) and a quest for illusion (epitomised in *el pan y el beso*). But in a Lorcan context an unbridled horse almost inevitably leads to death (cf. the warning to Soledad Montoya: *caballo que se desboca / al fin encuentra la mar / y se lo tragan las olas*), especially when there is accompanying lamentation as in lines 3–4. The personified involvement of wind and windows serves to elevate and intensify both mystery and lamentation and the *llanto oscuro / del caballero* echoes Soledad's *pena negra*. Don Pedro's search for illusion, one feels, is similarly condemned. With apparently simple words Lorca has prepared his reader, both factually and emotively, for a characteristically doomed quest.

13–23. In a more prosaic and realistic context one might here expect an explanation of Don Pedro's sorrows. Instead, a lake interrupts the narration, with a subtle interplay of new resonances and line-lengths suggestive of *canciones* rather than *romances*. The tone too changes. Now it is playful and teasing, with a magical, childlike vision of the moon bathing in the lake and rousing the envy of the distant moon that it reflects. Appropriately it is a child who tells the night to clash the cymbals (the two moons). But a *laguna* is not only a lake; it is also a lacuna or gap in a manuscript and this meaning too is relevant. Hence the intentional loss of narrative. But loss of narrative has been seen by twentieth-century enthusiasts of the *romance* less as a defect than as a potential merit, a means of liberating the reader's imagination. 'Lo inacabado tiene un profundo encanto', wrote Azorín in an article on traditional *romances* (1915; *OC* III, 183), and Spain's greatest authority on the *romance*, Ramón Menéndez Pidal, whom Lorca accompanied in 1920 in search of oral *romances* in Granada, repeatedly emphasised the traditional *romance*'s fragmentary character, its 'saber callar a tiempo', as one of its greatest appeals. Lorca shared this view, deliberately played down narrative in his own *romances* and here, with impishness appropriate to the title, shows his main narrative disrupted

3. A cazar va el rey Don Pedro,
   a cazar como solía;
   le diera el mal de la muerte,
   para casa se volvía.
   A la entrada de la puerta
   vio un pastor que le decía: [. . .]
       (*RVC* III, 110).

— and submerged — by the *primera laguna*. The accompanying child-like vision epitomises the magic of unleashed imagination.

24–37. Time has passed and Don Pedro has reached a distant city of gold, surrounded by a forest. Various identifications have been proposed (Medina Sidonia, Seville, Jerusalem). But more important, perhaps, than any specific identification is the echo of countless legends and fairy tales and stories of knightly quest. 'Only one castle is there in this wood,' says Wolfram von Eschenbach's Sigune to Parzifal. 'In it does every wish find its fulfilment.' It is in this light, I suggest, that Don Pedro's own *bosque*-surrounded golden city should be seen — and felt: as a mythical object of illusion.[2] Lorca's own *¿Es Belén?* seems to confirm the suggestion: the city is akin to Bethlehem but not immediately identifiable with it. Scents and brightness suggest further illusion — with further legendary echoes —, but are muted by a pointer to ruin (*arcos rotos*) and by funereal *velones de plata* borne by unidentified persons who again recall half-forgotten tales and increase the impression of mystery and ill omen.[3] We are poised, then, characteristically in a Lorcan context, between illusion and disillusion. Poplars and nightingale take up and confirm the duality.

[2] Josephs and Caballero apply Valente's finding on 'Canción de jinete' to these lines and suggest the influence of Lord Dunsany's mythical Carcassonne, 'con el sol brillando sobre su ciudadela en la cima de una lejana montaña' (293). Specific influence is unlikely, for Dunsany's work was not published in Spain until 1924. But the similarity is therefore — for me at least — all the more suggestive. Dunsany's castle (a clear echo of Wolfram's Schastel Merveille) is but another incarnation of man's quest for illusion. Marcilly's advocacy of Jerusalem, too, is relevant ('Ville d'or [. . .] que Josèphe compare à un soleil éblouissant au sommet d'une montagne de neige') but not admissible, I suggest, as a unique explanation, with the exclusion of other resonances.

[3] Compare, for example, the *pastor* in the third example quoted above in Note 1 and the *pastorico* who later appears in the first *romance* quoted, 'llorando y gimiendo, / la cabeza desgreñada', with a fatal message for Don Pedro. Without of course suggesting specific influence I quote also from a single page of Ernest Newman's long survey of the legends that underlie Wagner's *Parsifal*: '[Chrétien's] Perceval arrives at a castle in which is an old king who, by reason of sickness, cannot rise from his couch [. . .]. A squire passes through the hall in front of the couch [. . .], bearing a lance down the shaft of which runs a trickle of blood. Two other squires follow with lighted candles; after them comes a maiden carrying a "graal" of

38–45. The narrative is submerged in a further *laguna* (in both senses of the word). It is less joyous than the first and the surface is now rippled. But a magical circle of birds and flames recalls the moon's reflection and similarly suggests released imagination, while witnesses amidst the bordering reed-beds are aware of the missing material. But there is another layer of meaning and an impressive unifying image that has hitherto been overlooked. In 1921, when he wrote this poem, Lorca was writing also his *Poema del cante jondo*. In it the guitar plays an important part and is much associated with dreams and yearning and lamentation. The strings are seen as six dancing maidens (I, 217), the sound hole as the eye of Polyphemus (I, 217) and the body of the guitar as a 'negro / aljibe de madera' (I, 191). The imagery of the *segunda laguna* is similar: the ripples suggest strings, the circle of birds and flames is 'El sollozo de las almas / perdidas, / [que] se escapa por su boca / redonda' (I, 191) and the lake itself, with its contained mystery (*sueño concreto y sin norte*, since unlike the river it does not flow), is the body of the guitar (the 'negro aljibe de madera' that weeps 'flecha sin blanco', I, 158). The *laguna*, then, is here seen as a guitar, akin to the cymbals of the *primera laguna* and similarly suggestive of resonances unleashed by the absence of narration. On one level the *testigos* may be scholars like Menéndez Pidal *que conocen lo que falta*, but on the more important evoked plane of the guitar they suggest fellow *aficionados* who surround the performer and are similarly aware of the underlying causes of sorrow.

46–63. The pathos increases. Characteristically Lorca does not in-dicate, by means of definite articles, that the *dos mujeres y un viejo* are the same as in lines 33–4; he merely suggests it by repetition and parallelism (cf. above, comment on *un niño* in 1:32). And because of this parallelism we are obliged to associate *van al cementerio* (49) with *le salen al encuentro* (35). Though certain critics deny it (because of the

pure gold, set with precious stones, which emits a dazzling light [...]. [Per-ceval] rides away in sore perplexity. Soon he meets with a lady who [...] upbraids him [...]. Later he encounters another woman [...]; she too reproaches him violently' (*Wagner Nights*, London 1949, p. 676). It is in such a context that Don Pedro's adventures — and Lorca's poem — can best be appreciated. Knightly romance is arguably more relevant to Lorca's 'Burla ...' than the *romance* form itself. The subtitle 'Romance con lagunas' may thus contain a double word-play and *burla*: not only in *lagunas* but also in *romance*.

ending of the poem) it is surely Don Pedro that the *dos mujeres y un viejo* — and we — expect to find in the graveyard. This impression is reinforced by the reference to his dead horse, and pathos is intensified by a lamb-like bleating in heaven and by the legendary and mythical unicorn whose only horn is shattered. Now the city of illusion is ablaze and an unidentified man goes off weeping *tierras adentro* (traditional echoes that have been much exploited in surrealist and expressionist painting). The last words are especially effective with their broadening of perspectives and the progression continues in the following lines with a cinema-like shift of focus to suggest cosmic detachment from Don Pedro's own failed quest and the reaffirmation of life's persistent duality of illusion (the star to the north) and questing traveller (the sailor to the south).

64–9. The words now are at rest beneath the water: the sediment of successive generation of stories like Don Pedro's (as in palimpsests which Lorca both referred to, III, 580, and sought to recreate in his poetry, I, 259–63). On a faded flower (*enfriada* in contrast to the earlier *llama*) that will likewise be fused with the *limo* beneath, Don Pedro, with a deflating and ironic *¡ay!*, is a forgotten playmate of frogs. His quest is over and cymbals and guitar are hushed. Only the croaking, it seems, will remain. But one may recall the fairy tale of the frog released from its spell by a princess's kiss and turned back into a prince. Certainly this is relevant to Lorca's concept of the *romance*. Like cymbals and guitar Don Pedro's adventure will resound in the lacunae of countless future tales of quest.

Certain references are insufficiently explained in the above outline. The name of the protagonist himself, for example, may suggest a specific reference worthy of clarification. Who is he and what is his quest? Anecdote, said Lorca, is unimportant in itself, 'pero da con su hilo invisible *unidad* al poema' (III, 243–4). If one can identify Don Pedro other elucidations may follow. Three main hypotheses have been proposed: that he is the Knight of Olmedo, that he is Saint Peter and that he is Peter the Cruel. Since the total length of the relevant studies is akin to that of the present book, I must here confine myself to a brief indication that the reader can follow up for himself.

1. *The Knight of Olmedo*. Developing an early suggestion by Díaz-Plaja, Glasser recalls both the historical basis of the popular song 'El caballero de Olmedo' and various elaborations on the theme, most notably Lope de Vega's play which reveals similarities to Lorca's poem

and allegedly throws light on the narrative that underlies Lorca's dreamlike fusion of fantasy and reality. The author makes some good points but the evidence is not wholly convincing. Nor is it clear that the identifying of Don Pedro with the knight of Olmedo (Don Miguel in history; Don Alonso in Lope's play) helps to solve specific difficulties in Lorca's poem. Most suggestive perhaps is Glasser's reference to the burlesque tradition of Don Bueso *romances* as a possible influence on Lorca's treatment.

2. *The Apostle Saint Peter*. This is strongly argued by Marcilly in the longest and most detailed commentary on any Lorcan *romance*. Poems in *Romancero gitano*, he reminds us, are significantly placed and the 'Tres romances históricos' form a final triptych. Since the first is based on Christian martyrology and the third on the Old Testament, it is difficult not to conclude that the second will be based on the New Testament. Don Pedro, he believes, is Saint Peter. The obvious biblical references (*el pan y el beso, Belén* ...) and the three lakes (also 'trois failles') as an echo of Peter's triple denial of Christ offer initial confirmation. In referring to the saint as *Don* Pedro, he continues, Lorca was simply parodying a medieval tradition (examples in Berceo: even 'Don Christo') and his ironic treatment of the cowardly apostle recalls Quevedo's own satirical treatment. According to Marcilly, then, Lorca reconstructs the apostle's movements between his denial of Christ (John 18:25–7) and his reappearance, together with John, as Mary Magdalene calls them both to the empty sepulchre (John 20:2). This is all modestly described as hypothesis and is followed by an extensive line-by-line commentary on the poem: the evocation of grief following the denial, the quest for the bread and kiss of Christ, the horse with its echo of the grace-bringing horse of the Apocalypse, the mystery of the Holy Word faithfully preserved in the water of the lake, the child who represents Christianity in its infancy and dreams of the union of the primitive Church on earth with the Church in heaven (*¡Noche; toca los platillos!*) .... Biblical references are offered to explain specific difficulties too: the *ciudad de oro* (Jerusalem), the cedars (much used in construction), *dos mujeres y un viejo* (the two Marys and Joseph of Arimathea) .... Finally, in the disillusioned and deflating ending of the poem Marcilly finds a pointer to Lorca's own disillusion with Christainity and an anticipation of his poem 'Crucifixión'. Not all his evidence and arguments are equally convincing and one may feel special doubt about the dense religious symbolism that he finds in the *lagunas*, 'la clef du poème', especially since he overlooks the essential key, the *burla* of Lorca's word-play on

lagunas and its relevance both to the traditional *romance* and to his own concept of poetry. But Marcilly's case is strong and can be further strengthened by two complementary pieces of evidence that he does not cite: Lorca's frequent references to the Passion elsewhere in *Romancero gitano* and the difficulty of the poem. As was pointed out in an earlier commentary, Lorca, as though fearing accusations of blasphemy or sacrilege, tended to be at his most arcane when exploiting biblical material.

3. *Peter the Cruel*. Gauthier sees Lorca's poem as a burlesque gloss on the 'Romance del rey don Pedro' alluded to above (Note 1), with the king who abandoned his young wife immediately after their marriage presented, with characteristic imagery, as a typically Lorcan impotent male and his wife, Doña Blanca, as a sexually unfulfilled female. Thus the golden city is Medina Sidonia where Doña Blanca was imprisoned, Bethlehem evokes the possibility of virgin birth, the *segunda laguna* ('le centre du drame') symbolises the two sexes, the *cementerio* points to *Yerma*-like fertility spells, the dead horse symbolises Don Pedro's lost virility .... Though the influence of the Don Pedro *romance* seems clear, Gauthier's declared Freudian interpretation of Lorca's poem is less convincing (see Marcilly, 34–5, for detailed criticism). Hernández too identifies Don Pedro with Peter the Cruel, reminds us that the king was closely associated with Seville and finds echoes of Seville in Lorca's poem (the *ciudad de oro*; the cedars and scented herbs; the reference to Bethlehem which suggests joyous *villancicos* akin to Lorca's view of Seville; finally, 'prueba concluyente', the line *Por el camino llano* which echoes a *sevillana* that Lorca later adapted for the Barraca: 'Camino de Sevilla / camino llano'). He recognises the probable influence of the *romance* referred to by Gauthier, but quotes also, in a different version, the *romancillo* that I cited in Note 1, together with two Galician *romancillos* that tell of an unnamed knight's request for help and lodging. He finds an antecedent too for the horse and reminds us that Peter the Cruel was known also as 'el Enamorado' and that Lorca jotted down the words 'Don Pedro enamorado' in the manuscript of the 'Romance del emplazado'.[4] The *dos mujeres*, he suggests, are the king's wife and his mistress, the *viejo* is a fusion of several possible characters and the *sí-*

---

[4] This point is further strengthened if one recalls that the *romance* that most influenced Lorca's 'Romance del emplazado' (above, p. 90) and the 'Romance del rey Don Pedro' are almost juxtaposed (nos. 64 and 66) in the famous Wolf-Menéndez Pelayo collection.

no duality (36–7) is a reflection of the King's dual personality .... The ultimate *burla*, he believes, is in the final lines where the protagonist ends up as a mere king of frogs (with an echo of Aesop's fable of the frogs who ask for a king). As in Marcilly's interpretation much — but not all — is convincing.

It is evident, says Marcilly, that his own interpretation and Gauthier's — and presumably Hernández's — are irreconcilable; Don Pedro is either Saint Peter or Peter the Cruel. On a purely anecdotic level this is true and, if one must choose, the overall weight of evidence will probably incline one to Marcilly's interpretation. But it was surely not from neglect — or even mere *burla* — that Lorca omitted a clear reference to underlying anecdote (cf. his intentionally mystifying *¿Es Belén?*). In this poem as elsewhere, I suggest, his aim was to avoid the fetters of a specific and narrowly circumscribed narrative and thereby to allow free rein to echoes and resonances, an aspect of the poem that Marcilly, with his emphasis on 'clarté' and his reservations about Lorca's own reference to the 'encanto poético indefinido de conversación borrada' (21, 26), somewhat neglects. Given the choice between this critic's rather rigid equation, Don Pedro = Saint Peter, and my own unidentified Don Pedro, a mythical legend- and fairy-tale-echoing Everyman oppressed by sorrow and questing for illusion that is ultimately denied, I should myself still be inclined to hold to the latter, both because it seems more Lorcan and because it explains better the powerful emotive impact of the poem. But this is not the choice. The two interpretations can be reconciled and perhaps must be reconciled in any adequate reading. Gauthier's and Hernández's evidence too is strong and at times, it seems, irrefutable. My suggestion, then, as with the remarkably similar 'Muerto de amor', is that Lorca's 'Burla ...' is intentionally multiple in its references and resonances, a revitalised *limo de voces perdidas*, embracing alike the profane (Peter the Cruel), the religious (Saint Peter) and, beyond this, Everyman. The same can be said of other elements besides Don Pedro and an example was offered in Note 2. In this multiplicity of reference and resonances lies, in part at least, the special appeal of the poem.

Select bibliography: M. Gauthier, 'Essai d'explication du romance con lagunas', in *LNL* 139 (October 1956), 1–23; C. Marcilly, *La "BDP ..." de FGL*, Paris 1957; D. M. Glasser, 'Lorca's "BDP ..."', in *Hispania* 47 (1964), 295–301; Loughran (1978), 157–62; Hernández, 35–46; Cobb (1983), 99–101; Lisboa, 225–50.

18

THAMAR Y AMNON

The Old Testament story of Amnon's rape of his half-sister Tamar is recounted in the second book of Samuel (13:1–22), has innumerable *romance* versions, was incorporated by Lope de Vega into his novel *Los pastores de Belén* and dramatised by Tirso de Molina in *La venganza de Tamar* and by Calderón in *Los cabellos de Absalón*. Lorca, we know, had read Calderón's play (I, lxvi) and was enthusiastic about Tirso's (Auclair). But it was the *romance* tradition — and especially the gypsy *romance* tradition — that he emphasised in his lecture-reading on *Romancero gitano* (III, 346) and, together with the Bible itself, it was doubtless this that influenced him most. 'Este poema,' he declared, 'es gitano-judío, como era Joselito, *el Gallo*, y como son las gentes que pueblan los montes de Granada y algún pueblo del interior cordobés.' 'Y de forma y de intención,' he continued, 'es mucho más fuerte que los desplantes de *La casada infiel*, pero tiene en cambio un acento poético más difícil, que lo pone a salvo de ese terrible ojo de guiña ante los actos inocentes y hermosos de la Naturaleza.' The combination of popular tradition and poetic difficulty is striking and, even more forcibly than elsewhere, confronts us with the problem of *popularismo* and *cultismo* in *Romancero gitano*. With its dense imagery, recondite references and wide resonances, 'Thamar y Amnón' is probably the most complex poem in the book. Because of this, and because reputable critics diverge more than elsewhere on specific points of interpretation, I am obliged to make greater use of brackets and footnotes than in earlier commentaries.

1–12. The moon turns over the parched lands while summer sows murmurs of tiger and flame. The *rumores de tigre y llama* may be the thunder and lightning of an approaching storm, but resonances are more important than mere equations. On the one hand, in the moon's turning, there is a suggestion of distance and detachment, perhaps also of infertility, since the moon is associated with the bringing of rain and here there is no rain;[1] on the other hand, in the summer's sowing, there is closeness and involvement, with a pointer to the potential fertility of rumblings, untamed animal and flame (all recurrent Lorcan images of

vitality). It is a characteristic duality, characteristically associated with
the world of nature.[2] Moreover, as comparison with the opening lines
of Poems 7, 9 and 16 shows, the syntax too is typically Lorcan, with the
juxtaposition of a main clause and a subordinate clause to present key
elements whose interplay, one assumes, will — characteristically again
— be elaborated in the course of the poem. But the immediately
following lines evoke an intermediate realm between heaven and
earth: above the roofs, where tension is suggested by resonant *nervios
de metal* with their superb multiplicity of meaning — nerves under
stress, steely sinews (as though bracing the universe) and sounding
harp — and a pathetic bleating of lambs is borne on the rippled air.[3]
The earth, it is suggested, is cracked by prolonged drought (*heridas
cicatrizadas*) while the storm's *luces blancas* act as cauteries (Hernández). More importantly, especially in view of what is to come, the
earth 'offers itself' (in contrast to the frigid moon) with signs already of
tigre animality in its scars and of *llama* passion in its searing light.
Thamar and Amnón have still to appear, but, by syntax, theme and

---

[1] Juan-Eduardo Cirlot, *Diccionario de símbolos*, 4th ed., Barcelona
1981, p. 283.

[2] Compare the interplay of night (impassive detachment) and day
(dynamic involvement) in the following complete poem, 'Balanza':

> La noche quieta siempre.
> El día va y viene.
> La noche muerta y alta.
> El día con un ala.
> La noche sobre espejos
> y el día bajo el viento (I, 279).

[3] Hernández sees the *nervios de metal* (6) as lightning, and on lines 7–8
López Castellón comments: 'El autor logra un efecto acertadísimo: aplica
al aire el rizado del pelo de las ovejas, y a los balidos de éstas lo cálido de su
lana.' It may well be so. But it is not always necessary to look for physical
justification in Lorca's imagery and less contoured resonances are in any
case more important. The immediate effect of the bleating, of course, is
of innocence and, in view of the parched earth, pathos. Beyond this,
comparison with the following lines is suggestive:

> Que al balido reciente y a la flor desnortada
> y a los senos sin huellas de la monja dormida
> responda negro toro de límites maduros
> con la flor de un momento sin pudor ni mañana (I, 965).

[contd.]

imagery, the contrast and conflict between them are already with us, in the initial setting of the poem.

13–36. To the accompaniment of cold tambourines and bemooned citherns (with echoes of the moon's detachment and a reminder of Preciosa's own *luna de pergamino* and associated purity) Thamar was dreaming (muted from *cantando* in an earlier draft) a bird-like song of innocent love (with a possible echoing of Tamar's song in *La venganza de Tamar*: 'pájaro alegre, / que viste la esperanza / de plumas y alas verdes', Díaz-Plaja). Her nakedness, with a suggestion of both coldness and enticement (18) that recalls the moon in Poem 1, seeks yet further coldness — begs snowflakes of her belly and hailstone of her shoulders — and five frozen doves encircle her feet.[4] One is reminded of the cherubs that traditionally encircle the feet of the Virgin in paintings of the Immaculate Conception (Zurbarán, Carreño, Antolínez, Murillo, Coello ...). But purity is here associated also with life-condemning frigidity and Loughran is probably justified in recalling the virginal chastity of Diana (Selene), the moon goddess (cf. above, 2:1–8). Amnón, in contrast, burns with sexual desire as he watches his sister from a tower (a tarot-pack pointer to the moon's inaccessibility).[5] Lines 29–32 pose a problem and critics and trans-

They are from 'Oda al Santísimo Sacramento del Altar', 'quizá el poema más grande que yo haya hecho' (1928; III, 982), and evoke the attraction of the devil, with his black-bull enticement of the innocent by offering immediate pleasure. The *balido de lana* in 'Thamar ...', I suggest, corresponds to the *balido reciente* in the 'Oda ...' and, together with the moon, prepares the way for Thamar, akin to the *monja dormida*. Amnón's own animal vitality, corresponding to the *negro toro*, is here heralded in the tiger, a potential predator on sheep in the same way that Amnón will be a predator on Thamar.

   [4] The usual interpretation is that she seeks cooling snowflakes *for* her belly and hailstone *for* her shoulders (cf. Cobb: 'Begs snowflakes for her belly *hot* / And hail for her bare arms'; my italics). Both syntactically and contextually I prefer the reading proposed above. Despite the heat, Thamar is associated throughout with moonlike coldness. The whiteness of her moon-bathed body seems to offer her the possibility of snowflakes and hailstone to maintain her frigidity against the heat (both real and metaphorical). The frozen doves reinforce this suggestion. So also, by contrast, do lines 49–52: Amnón's burning body under cool sheets.

   [5] Cirlot, 285. Since Cirlot writes without reference to Lorca, his findings are especially suggestive. Mention has already been made of his association

lators are divided about whether they refer to Amnón or Thamar. Since lines 13–24 describe Thamar, it is tempting to assume that 25–36 describe Amnón, pierced by Cupid's arrow, and this seems to be the majority view ('12 versos para Thamar e outros 12 para Amnón', Lisboa). But *Su desnudo* and *terraza* (29–30) echo the earlier description of Thamar (22) and *terraza* cannot easily be reconciled with the *torre* where Amnón is spying on his sister. An earlier draft of the poem makes this clearer, for *Su desnudo iluminado* and *terraza* (29–30) coexisted initially with *asomado a la ventana* (subsequently changed to the present line 34). Since these cannot refer to the same person and since *asomado* refers to Amnón, lines 29–30 must refer to Thamar; so also, by extension, must lines 31–2. As though wounded by her brother's piercing gaze Thamar no longer sings; the innocent *pájaros en su garganta* have given way to a doleful *rumor entre dientes*. The explicit naming of Amnón in line 33, suggesting a change of subject, reinforces this interpretation and further associates Thamar with the moon. The association continues in lines 33–6: *Amnón estaba mirando / la luna* echoes the child's fascinated gazing in Poem 1 (1:3–4) and the *pechos durísimos* recall the earlier moon's *senos de duro estaño* (1:8) — in short, with the same duality of seductiveness and frigidity. The relevance of all this to the distant, detached moon of lines 1–2 is obvious. Thamar appears as the human incarnation of lunar qualities that were there merely suggested. In contrast, we might suspect, Amnón will incarnate the sexuality of tiger and burning earth, and lines 27–8 have already pointed the way, both with their overt sexuality and with the echoing of *llena / de heridas cicatrizadas* in *llenas las ingles de espuma*.

of the moon with the bringing of rain. Among other relevant observations I note the following: 'cítara, símbolo cósmico; sus cuerdas corresponden a los planos del universo [. . .]; significa la integración del cielo y de la tierra' (133); the moon's feminine character (passivity) contrasted with the sun's masculine character ('actividad ardiente') and the representation of the marriage of heaven and earth as that of sun and moon (283–4); the tarot harpist (cf. 'Thamar . . .', 6, 100), a symbol of the soul, who sings to a girl in the moonlight, with an allusion to the moon's 'carácter mortuario' (285); 'pájaros que hablan y cantan, simbolizando los anhelos amorosos, igual que las flechas y los vientecillos' (350; cf. 'Thamar . . .', 14, 32, 63, where all three appear); finally, the 'esencia doble' of the fish: 'símbolo del sacrificio y de la relación entre el cielo y la tierra'; 'símbolo de la fecundidad' (360; cf. 'Thamar . . .', 65–6).

37–68. In lines 13–36 a succession of descriptive present and imperfect tenses was stopped short by the preterite *vio* which thus appeared as a culminating revelation and incentive to action. It is this action with which we are concerned in lines 37–68 and it begins appropriately with a specific indication of time and a further preterite. Characteristically in Lorca, human suffering — in this case Amnón's torment of unrequited desire — is communicated to the world around and the room where he lies is wounded by his eyes (an echo of the *flecha recién clavada*) which, as though prompted by the earlier *alero*, take flight to visions of his sister's nakedness. The light outside is solid and oppressive (41–2), with only subdued pointers to life (43–4), and water, Lorca's most persistent image of life and vitality, is triply muted in line 45 (cultist *linfa; de pozo; oprimida*) and reveals itself only in silence.[6] The biblical serpent is recalled in lines 47–8, with stress on the two words that most clearly associate it with Thamar's enticing nakedness: *tendida* (cf. 30) and *canta* (cf. 21). But in contrast to the girl's coldness of *copos* and *granizo* amidst the surrounding heat, Amnón's flesh, under cooling sheets, is *quemada*, with trickles of perspiration. In the Bible story Tamar was lured to Amnon's room by a ruse and raped. Lorca's poem is more ambiguous. There is no indication of ruse and Thamar's silent entry into a silenced room might suggest complicity. Besides, both her earlier nakedness and the associated *cobra tendida canta* suggest woman's temptation of man and this is further recalled in *turbia de huellas lejanas*, with an apparent reminder of Eve's temptation of Adam. But, like the moon in Poem 1, Thamar combines seductiveness with frigidity, and pointers to her coldness and unyielding remoteness (55, 58) continue to contrast with the heat of Amnón's

[6] Cf. 'A garden inclosed is my sister, my spouse; a spring shut up, a fountain sealed' (Song of Solomon 4:12). In the context of Lorca's poem line 45 points to repressed vitality akin to that of Amnón. The biblical reference could suggest relevance also to Thamar. This fits in well with what is to come — and with Lorca's notion of the passions that burn under self-imposed restraint and apparent frigidity (cf. above, introduction to the commentary on 'La monja gitana').

[7] The *dos peces* recall the vitality of the fish-filled night in 'Preciosa y el aire' (another poem of sexual threat) and Cirlot, without reference to Lorca, has noted that the fish is a traditional symbol of sacrifice and of the relationship of heaven and earth (360). Relevant too — here as elsewhere — is the biblical tone of much of Lorca's imagery: for example, 'Thy two breasts are like two young roes that are twins' (Song of Solomon 7:3).

passion (59–60) and the contrast is echoed in Thamar's words to her brother (61–4). Amnón's reply reaffirms the duality of his sister's inaccessibility (*pechos altos*) and enticement (*dos peces que me llaman*).[7] But he senses also the *rumor* of suppressed vitality (cf. 4, 31). Thamar's lunar enticement and Amnón's earthy passion, it seems, are here close to cosmic union.

69–76. Characteristically nature responds to the event: first with the neighing of horses; then with its own interplay of contained passion (*sol en cubos*; cf. Thamar's *rumor de rosa encerrada*) and insistent fertility (traditionally associated with the vine: *delgadez de la parra*; cf. Amnón, *delgado y concreto*). The violence of the sexual act itself (73–6) is expressed first in the sort of language that one most commonly associates with the traditional *romance*, direct and specific, with relevance only to Thamar and Amnón (73–4);[8] then through sophisticated metaphorical language, with wider resonances and characteristic ambiguity (75–6). The streams traced by the *corales tibios* point to lacerations of Thamar's flesh. But more important is their warmth and colour which contrast with the former cold and whiteness of her body (*copos* and *granizo*, 19–20). They also recall earlier pointers to laceration and fertility: the tiger's sowing (3–4), the wounds of the earth in its surrender (9–10), the *transitorio / coral de rosas y dalias* amidst the *arena parda* (42–4). Finally, they echo Amnón's own passionate *hilos de sangre* (59) and appear as streams on a map. In Thamar's wounds, it seems, we are invited to find, as in Olalla's, a new fertility. Thamar's lunar frigidity has been violated; the *rosa encerrada* released; the 'monja dormida' awakened. With cosmic significance it is as though, in the overall context of the book, the moon that was victorious in her seductiveness in Poem 1 has now been brought down to earth and her cold purity finally overcome.

77–92. *Por encima de las casas* cries shatter the earlier harmony, *por encima de los techos*, of sounding *nervios de metal* (5–6). It is not clear whether they are Thamar's cries or the cries of people responding to the event. The ambiguity is probably intentional, for the following six lines too seem to bring together both echoes of the rape and pointers to a wider response: dagger and torn tunic (recalling the wounds and shift

---

[8] Cf. La cogió por los cabellos,
     la arrastró por la sala (cit. Alvar).

in 74–5) but now in the plural (with echoes of wounds and biblical
garments rent in anguish);[9] slaves going up and down stairways (more
external but still with sexual connotations, especially in view of the
accompanying *puñales* and *émbolos y muslos*; finally, a futurist image
of throbbing pistons and thighs (obviously sexual but with an
accompanying indication of nature's stunned response, *bajo las nubes
paradas*). Around Thamar, with pointers to a gypsy marriage custom
(the piercing of the hymen to confirm virginity), shrieking gypsy virgins
collect the drops of her deflowered maidenhood.[10] And as white cloths
turn red (with blood) in the closed rooms, vine-shoots and fish (cold
half-light, with echoes also of the sexual act, 66, 72) are similarly
transformed by the warmth and vitality of the new day.

93–100.   As Amnón flees on his pony, guards fire arrows at him from
walls and watchtowers.[11] And as the hoofbeats faded into the distance
David cut the strings of his harp. When the lines are read with
adequate awareness of relevant context their effect is devastating. But
no critic has so far pointed to either of the two most important aspects
of relevant context. The first is external to the poem. The second book
of Samuel tells not only of Amon's rape of Tamar; it tells also, two
chapters previously, of David's taking of Bathsheba, the wife of Uriah
the Hittite: 'And it came to pass in an eveningtide, that David arose
from off his bed, and walked upon the roof of the king's house: and
from the roof he saw a woman washing herself; and the woman was
very beautiful to look upon [. . .]. And David sent messengers, and

[9] Compare Tamar in the Bible story (13:19) and later, after the
death of Amnon, King David and his servants: 'Then the king arose,
and tare his garments, and lay on the earth; and all his servants stood
by with their clothes rent' (13:31).

[10] The custom is celebrated in the following gypsy bridal song:

> En un verde prado
> tendí mi pañuelo;
> salieron tres rosas
> como tres luceros (cit. Alvar).

[11] As with the rent clothes Lorca's lines have biblical resonances but the
specific situation has been changed. In the Bible story Amnon does not
flee; nor is he shot at from the walls. But both these things appear in
associated episodes from the same second book of Samuel: 'all the king's
sons arose, and every man gat him upon his mule, and fled' (13:29); 'And
the shooters shot from off the wall upon thy servants' (11:24).

took her; and she came in unto him, and he lay with her' (11:2–4). This, I suggest, was Lorca's source for lines 13–36, for there is nothing comparable in the biblical story of Tamar and Amnon. Add to this, God's anger at David's action ('Thus saith the Lord, Behold, I will raise up evil against thee out of thine own house', 12:11) and Lorca's concern with heredity, fate and retribution, and one understands why he fused the two: Amnón's rape of Thamar is a decreed re-enactment of David's rape of Bathsheba. The King's cutting of the strings of his harp is a despairing recognition of the foretold retribution, evil raised up against him out of his own house. The other most important piece of relevant context is internal and depends on a proper understanding of the resounding *nervios de metal* in line 6. In their immediate context they suggested steely sinews, over the housetops, bracing the realms of moon and earth in cosmic harmony; also, less obviously, harp strings (cf. 'El arpa y su lamento / prendido en nervios de metal dorado', I, 959). Now, in retrospect, this subsidiary meaning takes on its full significance, but the higher meaning is not therefore lost. Besides, the words just quoted are significantly from a poem dedicated to the supreme poet of cosmic harmony, Fray Luis de León. David's final cutting of the harp strings signifies not only an end to his playing — and an appropriate end to *Romancero gitano* —; it is also a despairing acknowledgement of retribution fulfilled and a recognition of cosmic harmony destroyed. Read in this light, I repeat, the final lines of the poem are devastating.

Relatively little critical guidance is available. Díaz-Plaja emphasises the influence of Tirso de Molina's *La venganza de Tamar* (with comments on stylistic differences) and Alvar the popular *romance* tradition (with a fascinating complementary study on early elaborations of the Bible story in Spanish oral tradition, *op. cit.*, 163–237). Schonberg and Auclair are enthusiastic about the poem ('le plus puissant de tous'; 'le chef-d'œuvre de [l']ensemble') but modest in justifying their enthusiasm. Correa too says little — surprisingly, for in its cosmic dimension and imagery this poem supports his general thesis better than any other in *Romancero gitano*. López Castellón offers a brief, Cobb a fuller and Lisboa the fullest general survey, without really getting to grips with the poem. Hernández's study of sound imagery, with special reference to musical instruments and musical sounds, takes on greater significance in the light of my above emphasis on cosmic harmony. Loughran comes closest to my own approach in his emphasis on cosmic significance but interprets differently: the poem, he suggests, is 'a mythical allegory of dawn', a conflict between the moon (Thamar/Diana) and the sun (Amnón/Apollo), with the final victory of the latter as dawn appears.

Select bibliography: Díaz-Plaja, 135–9; Schonberg, 199–202; Correa, 47–8; M. Alvar, *El romancero: tradicionalidad y pervivencia*, Barcelona 1970, pp. 240–5 ('GL en la encrucijada' [1959]); M. Auclair, *Enfances et mort de GL*, Paris 1968, pp. 173–8; Loughran (1972), 260–7; Hernández, 32–4; Cobb (1983), 101–4; Lisboa, 253–67; López Castellón, 22.

SELECT BIBLIOGRAPHY

Emphasis is on works helpful for the comprehension and appreciation of individual poems. Studies chiefly relevant to a single poem are not listed here, but a selection is included in the more specific end-of-commentary bibliographies. General studies on *Romancero gitano* are reserved for the bibliography in my edition of the text. Abbreviations: (F)GL, (Federico) García Lorca; *RG. Romancero gitano; A* I, *Autógrafos*, I (the third item below); *RVC, Romances viejos castellanos* (details on p. 19); UP, University Press; those referring to periodicals are in accordance with *The Year's Work in Modern Language Studies*; those of poem titles (in the end-of-commentary bibliographies) are obvious in context.

BASIC TEXTS

Federico García Lorca, *Obras completas*, Madrid: Aguilar, 22nd ed., 3 vols., 1986 [Unless otherwise stated, Lorca page references are to this edition].

——, 'Romancero gitano' [1935–36], in *OC* III, 339–46 [Lorca's own invaluable commented reading].

——, *Autógrafos*, I (*Facsímiles de ochenta y siete poemas y tres prosas*), ed. Rafael Martínez Nadal, Oxford: Dolphin, 1975 [Facsimiles and transcription of pre-publication manuscripts, at times only fragmentary; includes, in part at least, *RG* poems 1, 5, 6, 7, 9, 10, 13, 14, 15, 16, 18; hereafter abbreviated *A* I].

TRANSLATIONS INTO ENGLISH

——, *Poems*, trans. Stephen Spender and J. L. Gili, London: Dolphin, 1939 [includes *RG* 4, 6, 12, 18].

——, *Gypsy Ballads*, trans. Langston Hughes, in *The Beloit Poetry Journal* II, Chapbook no. 1 (Fall 1951) [*RG* 1–15].

The Gypsy Ballads of FGL, trans. Rolfe Humphries, Bloomington: Indiana UP [1953], 3rd printing 1963 [All 18 poems].

Lorca, trans. J. L. Gili, Harmondsworth: Penguin, 1960 [Includes prose translations of *RG* 1, 3, 4, 5, 6, 7, 10, 11, 12, 14, 15, 18].
——, *Gipsy Ballads*, trans. Michael Hartnett, Dublin: The Goldsmith Press, 1973 [*RG* 1–15, with omissions].
See also below, especially Cobb 1983.

COMMENTARY-BASED STUDIES (with or without translation; in chronological order of first publication)

Guillermo Díaz-Plaja, *FGL* [1948], Buenos Aires: Austral, 1954, pp. 37–56, 106–40 [Comments on all *RG* poems].

C. M. Bowra, *The Creative Experiment*, London: Macmillan, 1949, pp. 189–219 [Brief comments on most *RG* poems].

Roy Campbell, *Lorca. An Appreciation of his Poetry*, Cambridge: Bowes & Bowes, 1952, pp. 20–4, 40–61 [Good renderings into ballad metre (though often only extracts); brief comments on most *RG* poems].

Jean-Louis Schonberg, *FGL. L'homme. L'œuvre*, Paris: Plon, 1956, pp. 186–211 [Brief comments on all *RG* poems].

Gustavo Correa, *La poesía mítica de FGL*, Eugene: Oregon UP, 1957, pp. 22–53 [Myth-emphasising commentaries on all *RG* poems].

Fernando Vázquez Ocaña, *GL. Vida, cántico y muerte*, Mexico: Grijalbo, 1957, pp. 212–35 [Much *RG* quotation; brief comments].

Albert Henry, *Les grands poèmes andalous de FGL*, Ghent: Romanica Gandensia 6, 1958, 217–46 [Comments on most *RG* poems].

Lore Terracini, 'Acerca de dos romances gitanos', in *QIA* 4 (1958), 429–43 [On the different effect of the 'triple reiteración' in *RG* 1 (*luna, luna, luna*) and 8 (*monte, monte, monte*)].

John Frederick Nims, 'FGL', in *The Poem Itself* [1960], ed. Stanley Burnshaw, Harmondsworth: Penguin, 1964, pp. 232–50 [Translation and commentary; *RG* 2, 4, 6, 7].

Josette Blanquat, 'La lune manichéenne dans la mythologie du *RG*', in *RLC* 38 (1964), 376–99 [Emphasises *RG* 1 and 14].

Howard T. Young, *The Victorious Expression*, Madison: Wisconsin UP, 1964, pp. 164–80 [Text and translation with brief comment: *RG* 1, 2, 4].

Carl W. Cobb, *FGL*, New York: Twayne, 1967, pp. 58–78 [Comments on all *RG* poems].

Francisco Umbral, *Lorca, poeta maldito*, Madrid: Biblioteca Nueva, 1968, pp. 95–125 [Reflections — usually psychological or sociological — on most *RG* poems].

Emilia de Zuleta, *Cinco poetas españoles* [1971], 2nd ed., Madrid: Gredos, 1981, 257–68 [Includes comments on *RG* 7, 11, 12, 15].

David Loughran, 'Myth, the gypsy, and two *romances históricos*', in *MLN* 87 (1972), 253–71 [Comments on *RG* 1, 2, 10, 15; commentaries on 16 and 18].

Carlos Feal Deibe, *Eros y Lorca*, Barcelona: EDHASA, 1973, pp. 63–71, 129–228 [*RG* 1, 2, 3, 6, 8, 11 and 12 on the Freudian couch].

Trinidad Durán Medina, *FGL y Sevilla*, Seville: Diputación Provincial, 1974 [Commentaries on *RG* 10 and 11; briefer comment on *RG* 12].

Allen Josephs and Juan Caballero (eds.), FGL, *Poema del cante jondo*, *RG*, Madrid: Cátedra, 1977, pp. 225–302 [Erudite footnotes to all *RG* poems].

María Andueza, *Once poemas comentados de FGL*, Mexico: Universidad Nacional Autónoma, 1978, pp. 43–70 [Commentaries on *RG* 1, 4, 13].

David Loughran, *FGL. The Poetry of Limits*, London: Tamesis, 1978, pp. 135–63 [Commentaries on *RG* 2, 5, 7, 11, 12, 14, 15, 16, 17].

Bonnie Shannon McSorley, 'Nature's sensual and sexual aspects in three gypsy ballads of GL', in *The World of Nature in the Works of FGL*, ed. J. W. Zdenek, Rock Hill, South Carolina: Winthrop Studies, 1980, pp. 81–9 [*RG* 1, 2, 4].

Derek Harris, 'The theme of the Crucifixion in Lorca's *RG*', in *BHS* 58 (1981), 329–38 [With special reference to *RG* 10, 11, 12, 17].

Mario Hernández (ed.), Introduction to FGL, *RG*, Madrid: Alianza [1981], 2nd ed., 1983, pp. 9–46 [Commentary on *RG* 17; comments on *RG* 18].

Miguel García-Posada (ed.), Introduction to FGL, *Poesía*, 2, Madrid: Akal, 1982, pp. 11–41 [Includes brief comments on all *RG* poems].

Carl W. Cobb, *Lorca's 'RG'. A Ballad Translation and Critical Study*, Jackson: Mississippi UP, 1983 [All *RG* poems: translation and commentary].

José Carlos Lisboa, *Verde que te quero verde (Ensaio de interpretação do 'RG' de GL)*, Rio de Janeiro: Zahar, 1983 [Extensive commentary on all *RG* poems].

Enrique López Castellón (ed.), Introduction to FGL, *RG* . . . , Madrid: Busma, 1983, pp. 9–23 [Comments briefly on all *RG* poems].

Luis Beltrán Fernández de los Ríos, *La arquitectura del humo: una reconstrucción del 'RG' de FGL*, London: Tamesis, 1986 [Expansive commentary on all *RG* poems].

Andrew P. Debicki, 'Metonimia, metáfora y mito en el *RG*', in *CHA* 435–6 (September–October 1986), 609–18 [With special reference to *RG* 3, 6 and 15].

Post–1985 publications have in general not been incorporated into the more specific end-of-commentary bibliographies.

Lorca's *Romancero gitano*

This poem-by-poem guide to Lorca's *Romancero gitano* was prompted by the need for some form of guidance to the overwhelming amount of critical material published on the book, the relative neglect or misunderstanding of certain poems, and a concern to counter a recent tendency to eccentric interpretation. Herbert Ramsden's comprehensive collection of commentaries will be useful both for students and teachers and for the Lorca specialist. With each poem the author offers a brief introduction to relevant background material, a comprehensive commentary, a brief indication of interpretations notably different from his own, and a select critical bibliography. In a more general bibliography the author lists a number of translations of *Romancero gitano* into English and a selection of commentary-based studies. The great diversity and allusive richness of Lorca's poetic masterpiece demands more space than a compact study edition allows, and all serious students of *Romancero gitano* will want to use Herbert Ramsden's *Eighteen commentaries* alongside his simultaneously-published edition of the text.

H. Ramsden is Emeritus Professor of Hispanic Studies at the University of Manchester.

Spanish texts

This distinguished series seeks to meet the needs of today's school and university students with short modern works by leading Spanish and Latin American authors. The basic format – text in Spanish accompanied by introduction, bibliography, notes and glossary in English – remains but has been redesigned for maximum conciseness and ease of use.

Antona García Tirso de Molina ed. M. Wilson

La vida de Lazarillo de Tormes ed. R. O. Jones

Bodas de sangre García Lorca ed. H. Ramsden

La casa de Bernarda Alba García Lorca ed. H. Ramsden

Romancero gitano García Lorca ed. H. Ramsden

El coronel no tiene quien le escriba García Márquez ed. G. Pontiero

San Manuel Bueno, mártir and La novela de don Sandalio Miguel de Unamuno ed. A. Longhurst

The cover illustration is from García Lorca's title-page design for *Romancero gitano*

Manchester University Press

Manchester and New York

Distributed exclusively in the USA and Canada by St. Martin's Press Inc., 175 Fifth Avenue, New York, NY 10010, USA

M.U.P. NET.
£ 6.95

0-7190-2849-3